C0-AVX-805

In Search
of a Crown

In Search
of a Crown

❧

HELEN B. EMMONS

✠

ABINGDON PRESS
New York   *Nashville*

IN SEARCH OF A CROWN

Copyright © MCMLVIII by Abingdon Press

All rights in this book are reserved.
No part of the book may be reproduced in any
manner whatsoever without written permission of
the publishers except brief quotations embodied in
critical articles or reviews. For information address
Abingdon Press, Nashville 2, Tennessee.

Library of Congress Catalog Card Number: 58-7430

B

SET UP, PRINTED, AND BOUND BY THE
PARTHENON   PRESS,   AT   NASHVILLE,
TENNESSEE, UNITED STATES OF AMERICA

DEDICATED TO
the shining memory of
CARLTON
who so early won the crown of life

Preface

Every little girl dreams of becoming queen of the May. She pictures herself seated upon a flower throne, wearing a wreath of May blossoms, watching the maypole dancers on the green before her.

The years pass and one day she secretly longs to be chosen queen of the football game, or even more to be the queen of the college home-coming day. Later on perhaps, she longs to enter the contest for the beauty pageant crown.

Gradually her dreams fade. The crowns she dreamed about were made of material things, such as paper, flowers, or even gold or precious stones. When the coronation is over they disappear. In time the beauty which earns them disappears too.

But there are crowns of another sort for you and me to wear, crowns which everyone may earn and which will not pass away. They are invisible crowns, seen only by the eyes of love, by the eyes of the soul.

J. H. Jowett was thinking of crowns such as these when he wrote:

I think I know many people who are already wearing the crowns in their hearts. It seems to me that there are many people from whom God has only to strip away their robes of flesh and they will stand before Him—crowned! They wear the crown of humility, the crown of patience, the crown of brotherly kindness, the crown of hope, the crown of love. Do you think anyone will be able to wear brighter crowns than these in the kingdom of God?

In these devotional services we will be seeking crowns. I hope that the meditations will be guideposts along the way of this search. The worship leader may read these meditations from the book if necessary. But I hope that the outline will be meaningful enough for her to go beyond the book and present the ideas in terms of her own experience.

For special days the following meditations may be used:

"A Crown of Life" for Easter
"A Crown of Thanksgiving" for Thanksgiving"
"A Crown of Wisdom" for Christmas

The hymns selected for the services may be found in most Protestant hymnals. The selections in poetry will be effective if given by other members on the program.

I wish to thank the publishers and copyright owners who have kindly given me permission to use copyright material, and to beg indulgence of any whose source of material I have been unable to find.

Most especially I thank my daughter, Mrs. Mary Emmons Worthington, for her gracious help and patience in typing the manuscript.

HELEN B. EMMONS

Contents

1. A Crown of Womanhood 13

2. A Crown of Jewels 21

3. A Crown of Beauty 29

4. A Crown of Devotion 37

5. A Crown of Thorns 45

6. A Crown of Life 52

7. A Crown of Witness 59

8. A Crown of Sorrow 65

9. A Crown of Gold 72

10. A Crown of Friendship 79

11. A Crown of Joy 84

12. A Crown of Love 91

13. A Crown of Contentment 99

14. A Crown of Thanksgiving 106

15. A Crown of Wisdom 112

16. A Crown of Hope 117

17. Wearing the Crown 123

CHAPTER I

A Crown of Womanhood

Scripture: Prov. 31:10-31

Hymns: "All Hail the Power of Jesus' Name"
"Happy the Home When God Is There"
"O Happy Home, Where Thou Art Loved the Dearest"

Meditation:

Speaking of womanhood, John Ruskin, in his famous "Sesame and Lilies," says:

Whether consciously or not, you must be, in many a heart, enthroned: there is no putting by that crown; queens you must always be; queens to your lovers; queens to your husbands and your sons; queens of higher mystery to the world beyond, which bows itself, and will forever bow, before the myrtle crown, and the stainless scepter of womanhood. But, alas! you are too often idle and careless queens, grasping at majesty in the least things, while you abdicate it in the greatest.

The gleam of this crown is found within the walls of a woman's own home and beside

13

her own fireside. She need not travel far in search of it. In the home a woman has always found her greatest influence and reward. God has given her talents that find their highest expression in homemaking and motherhood.

The Influence of a Christian Home

We can never forget our first home and the ones who presided over it. That home will always hold a special place in our hearts. The things we learned there are a part of us forever. Our hearts were soft and what we heard and saw there sank deep into the mold.

The fashion of those early experiences we weave into the fabric of the homes we found in later life. The stories our mother told us we tell to our children. The songs she sang to us we sing to them. The cherished traditions and customs of our childhood we follow in new homes of our own.

My father loved to sing. For over sixty years he sang in the church choir, even to the night before his death at eighty years. From the time we were little children until we were grown, he gathered us around the piano on Sunday evening to sing hymns with us. It became a part of our Sunday tradition. When my own children were growing up, we too sang around the piano. The habit lures me still.

14

Most of us will never be able to reform the world in any great degree, but we can build Christian homes founded upon love and righteousness. In these homes we may rear our children who will go out to serve and bless their world.

Leslie Weatherhead has said:

I meet a great many people who wish they had more influence in the world and think they don't count for much. But if from your home there comes, because of what you have been and done, a good man or a good woman, you will have done more for your nation, more for the true progress of mankind and more for God than many of those whose names are written on the scrolls of fame.

The Atmosphere of the Home

The influence of the home is largely determined by the atmosphere in the home. It is the spirit in the home that changes a house into a home.

Victor Hugo reminds us:

A house is built of logs and stone,
Of tiles and posts and piers;
A home is built of loving deeds
That stand a thousand years.

A dress will go out of style, a rug will wear out, fine china will break, but the loving smile, the sympathetic word, the brave overcoming of disappointment, the unselfish act, the wise example, create homes which build strong Christian character in boys and girls and men and women.

The beauty of a home does not come necessarily from its cost and elegance. One exquisite picture need cost but little, but it can feed the soul. A row of books beside an easy chair, flowers in a vase, a sense of lovely orderliness rest the heart.

John Henry Jowett describes this kind of home in these words:

Anyone can build an altar; it requires a God to provide the flame. Anybody can build a house; we need the Lord for the creation of a home. A house is an agglomeration of bricks and stones, with an assorted collection of manufactured goods; a home is the abiding-place of ardent affection, of fervent hope, of genial trust. There is many a homeless man who lives in a richly furnished house. There is many a fifteen-pound house in the crowded street which is an illuminated and beautiful home. The sumptuously furnished house may only be an exquisitely sculptured tomb; the scantily furnished house may be the very hearthstone of the eternal God. Now the Christian religion claims to be able to convert houses into homes, to supply the missing fire, and to bring an aspiring flame to the cold and chilling heap. The New Testament does not say very much about homes; it says a great deal about the things that make them. It speaks about life and love and joy and peace and rest! If we get a house and put these things into it, we shall have secured a home.[1]

The Hospitality of the Home

The atmosphere of a home is expressed in its gracious hospitality. We justify the beauty and comfort of a home when we share it with those who do not have homes of their own. Few experiences are more rewarding than sharing food and fellowship with others, especially when the friends may be those of another race and culture. Visitors from other lands help our children to understand that although people are different in dress, manners, and customs, in things that matter they are very much the same as we are.

There was a lovely girl from the Orient who came to this country to study. For two years she was a frequent visitor in our home. She gave us a new appreciation of her country's art, music, food, and customs, and her spiritual character was an inspiration to all of us.

All around us there are visitors from other

[1] From *My Daily Meditations.* Used by permission of Fleming H. Revell Co.

17

lands who can widen the horizons of our small world and enrich our lives. There are many who need our friendship and who would welcome an invitation to our homes and hearts.

Who can estimate the importance of a Christian home? Perhaps the words of William E. Gladstone sum it up well. While talking one day to Thomas de Witt Talmage about world problems, races, and creeds, he said: "There is but one question. Settle that and you settle all others. That question is Christianity, and it must be settled in the home. The homes of the people are the soul of the nation."

PRAYER:

Thou blessed Christ who didst come into the world to set men and women free from everything which limits them, lead us into a truer understanding of our high privilege as wives and mothers and daughters. Grant that we may be willing to accept joyfully the service in the home, with its drudgery, frustration, and monotony. Help us to transform it into a glorious opportunity for serving thee. May the goodness and love of God be shed abroad in our hearts and in our homes. We ask for Jesus' sake. AMEN.

THANKSGIVING FOR HOME

Lord, Thou has given me a cell
   Wherein to dwell,
A little house whose humble roof
   Is weather-proof. . . .
Low is my porch, as is my fate,
   Both void of state;
And yet the threshold of my door
   Is worn by th' poor,
Who hither come and freely get
   Good words, or meat. . . .
'Tis Thou that crown'st my glittering hearth
   With guileless mirth. . . .
All these, and better Thou dost send
   Me, to this end,
That I should render, for my part,
   A thankful heart.

ROBERT HERRICK

PRAYER FOR A LITTLE HOME

God send us a little home,
To come back to, when we roam—

Low walls and fluted tiles;
Wide windows, a view for miles;

Red firelight and deep chairs;
Small white beds upstairs;

Great talk in little nooks;
Dim colors, rows of books;

One picture on each wall;
Not many things at all.

God send us a little ground,
Tall trees standing round.

Homely flowers in brown sod,
Overhead, Thy stars, O God.

God bless thee, when winds blow,
Our home, and all we know! [2]

FLORENCE BONE

CHAPTER II

A Crown of Jewels

SCRIPTURE: I Sam. 3:1-10
Mark 10:13-16

HYMNS: "I Think When I Read That Sweet Story of Old"
"It Fell upon a Summer Day"
"Lord of Life and King of Glory"

MEDITATION:

Of all the crowns a woman may seek, the fairest is the crown of jewels seen in the sparkling eyes of a little child.

The mother of the famous Gracchi of Rome, one later a tribune of the Empire, and another a leader in Roman life, was asked by a visitor if she might see her ornaments. Pointing to her children just returning from school, she said, "These are my jewels."

Jewels are rare and costly. So our children are "pearls of great price." They exact a dear cost. But they are worth all that we have.

21

In the Face of a Little Child

Michael Fairless in *The Roadmender*, speaking of an old organ grinder, says, "He saw the face of a little child and looked on God." As truly as a little child brings God to us, so we must bring God to the little child. We must acquaint him early with his Heavenly Father and teach him to live in love and harmony in the world his Father has made for him. This is the parent's greatest joy and opportunity.

Anne Shannon Monroe says:

Mothers who have developed in their children a strong current of power for right action have little to fear for them out in the world. To the God-inspired mother each new child is a new channel of power, a channel through which more God-wisdom may flow out into the world, or more earth stupidity, which depends in a great measure on this first household, and this in turn—barring exceptional circumstances—depends in a great measure on her.

As Christian parents we are challenged today as never before in rearing our children strong in the Christian faith and life. We are primarily responsible for this spiritual training. The church and the school will make their contribution later, but the roots must always be in the home.

Planting the Seed

While it is true that religion is best "caught" by contact with its power in another life, it is still necessary to make a conscious effort to implant it in the hearts of children. It is not enough to expect them to catch it by association alone. Over and over again its truth must be written in their hearts.

Beautiful Bible stories, great hymns of the church, fine passages of scripture, prayer, attendance at Sunday school and church are all avenues by which religious growth comes.

The help and comfort God's Word has given me in meeting life led me to seek a way to implant it in the memory of my children. When my oldest boy was ten, I selected each week a meaningful verse or verses of scripture which we read and underlined in his Bible. Every night as I told him good night we repeated together this verse and talked about it. At the end of the week he knew the verse from memory and he wrote it in a booklet he had prepared for it. Gradually he acquired a store of precious truth which would always belong to him.

We are reminded of Susannah Wesley. One night she had been praying for her family. "At last," she says, "it came into my mind that I might do more than I do. I resolved to begin. I will take such proportion of time as I can best spare every night to discourse with each child by itself.''

What glorious results came from the keeping of this resolution! The child who lives in such an atmosphere will someday hear, as did the young Samuel, God's voice speaking to him. And he will respond with loving obedience.

Each One a Person

Children are born to go in different ways. Each child is his own individual self. It takes the keenest discernment and study to discover these differences and to find the key to their dispositions.

Ramsay MacDonald, once prime minister of England, in speaking of his wife Margaret, said:

Her little folks were treasures given to her to guard and protect, not to mould in her own image. They had personalities of their own, and inheritances of their own. They were individuals, and it was her duty, she thought, to enrich them by teaching them how to use their own talents and faculties. She seemed to say: ''I am at hand to hold and to help you if necessary, but I want you to develop your own selves so that when you are men and women you will be persons of free will and not creatures of circumstance.''

She believed in discipline, not the discipline of force, but of spiritual desire, of reasoned conduct, of moral control of emotion and appetite. The words she used in a letter telling her children that their grandmother had died were very significant, "We must try to comfort each other."

Like a Deepening Stream

Above all other influences in the spiritual training of children is the personality of the mother herself. It is the greatest force in shaping the life of her child. By close companionship, her own character flows like a stream into her children, hour by hour.

A mother said to her young son one day, "Today we must go to town and buy you a pair of shoes."

"But Mother," he objected, "I don't want to go to town to buy shoes. Do I have to go?"

"Yes," she said, "but after we buy the shoes you and I will spend the rest of the afternoon together."

"Let's get started as quick as we can after lunch so that we'll have more time to be together," came the startling reply.

We may best fit ourselves for this task by deepening our own spiritual lives through study and through daily association with God. God must be real in our own lives if he is to become real to our children.

"As a child," said someone, "I had a feeling that God and Jesus were such particular friends of Mama's, and were honored more than words can tell."

Let us then,

Go speak to Jesus first,
Then to the child. . . .
Go speak to Jesus; wait His answering word,
Then tell the trusting child, like one who comes
Transfigured from the mount of prayer.

To build strong healthy bodies, to train keen, alert minds, and to lift up fresh, eager spirits to God—this is to find the crown of jewels.

PRAYER:

O thou Friend of little children, help us to realize that life can bring no greater joy to us than the opportunity to lead a little child into thy friendship. Grant that we may live lives so true that in loving us they may be able to love thee. Help us to grow in love and patience and in wisdom that we may be saved from mistakes in training our children. May we be conscious daily of thy presence and guidance that we may ever live in God. So shall we be safe patterns for children's feet to follow. In the dear name of Christ we pray. AMEN.

WORDS TO A YOUNG MOTHER

Go daily to an altar, there to pray
  That you be worthy of the sacred task
Of Motherhood. Ask wisdom for the day,
  And heed the answer to the thing you ask
So soon a child's grave eyes will watch to see
  Life's meaning in your voice, your smile, your
     face.
Each moment you will make some memory
  That all the coming years will not erase.
You will engrave upon a young child's heart
  Deep lettered words, carved there for good or ill,
Oh, Mother, do you know how great a part
  You are to play, how much you will distill
Of truth and beauty in the empty cup
  That your child's hands will soon be holding up?

AUTHOR UNKNOWN

Co-workers we with Him! Were He to ask,
"Come star with me the spaces of my night,
Or light with me tomorrow's sunset slow,
Or fashion forth the crystals of my snow,
Or teach my sweet June-roses next to blow."
O rare beatitude! But holier task,
Of all His works of beauty fairest-high,
Is that He keeps for hands like ours to ply!
When He upgathers all His elements,
His days, His nights, whole eons of His June,
The Mighty Gardener of the earth and sky,
That to achieve towards which the ages roll,
We hear the Voice that sets the sphere a-tune—
"Help me, my comrades, flower this budding
  Soul!"

AUTHOR UNKNOWN

Thou Healer, Teacher, Comforter divine!
I could not love Thee with such tender love
Hast Thou not friendship for the children shown.
O, Jesus, this Thy title would I bear—
The sweetest, dearest name e'er given Thee—
As Friend of children would I too be known.

AUTHOR UNKNOWN

28

CHAPTER III

A Crown of Beauty

SCRIPTURE: Matt 6:26-30
               Ps. 104

HYMNS: "For the Beauty of the Earth"
        "This Is My Father's World"
        "O Worship the King"
        "The Spacious Firmament on High"

MEDITATION:

There is a crown waiting for us out in God's out-of-doors world. There is rapture in it. There is glory in it. It is a pathway that will lead us to God.

Jesus knew this crown and this path. From the time he was a boy playing in the fields to the time he walked the Judean roads, teaching and preaching, he loved the beauties of his Father's world. He loved the flowers, the trees, the birds, the sheep, the pearls of the sea. He used them to illustrate his teachings. He sought the quiet hillside and the lonely desert for communion with his Father. He fought his battles in the solitude of nature. He loved the silence of the stars, and the glory of the dawn. He sat by the water's edge to preach. Let us follow in his steps and find some of the treasures he found.

Let Us Learn to Love the Trees

From March until June the forest is in flower and wonders are found on every branch. Tiny buds huddle close together on every twig and then open into petals of delicate color. Summer days bring cool shadows under leafy shade. The rich pageantry of the autumn woods burns in flame on every hillside. And who can say that the bare branches of wintertime are not delicate etchings against a sky of gray?

> Forests are made for weary men,
> That they may find their souls again.
> And little leaves are hung on trees
> To whisper of old memories.
> And trails with cedar shadows black
> Are placed there just to lead men back
> Past all the pitfalls of success
> To boyhood's faith and happiness.
> Far from the city's craft and fraud,
> O, Forest, lead me back to God! [1]

I grew up in the redwood country. Before Charlemagne was crowned at Rome, even before the ancient city on the Tiber was founded, and a thousand years before the

---

[1] "Leading," Mary Carolyn Davies.

birth of Christ, these ancient sequoias lifted leafy hands to pray.

I never stood beneath these giant trees that I did not feel the hush of a great cathedral in my heart. I seemed to feel the majesty of the rolling centuries through which these sentinels stood. Trivial concerns fell away, and the calmness of eternal things stole into my being. God spoke in my heart.

Let Us Learn to Love Flowers

Tennyson said that if we could but understand the mystery of a single flower we should know what God and man is. We do know that back of the flower's botanical mystery there lies a power which draws us through its beauty to the One who created it. Kagawa writes:

> Strange that the spring has come
> On meadow and vale and hill,
> For here in the sunless slum
> My bosom is frozen still.
> And I wear the wadded things
> Of the dreary winter days.
> But out of the heart of this little flower
> God gazes into my face.[2]

A Frenchman who had displeased Napoleon was thrown into a dungeon. He seemed to be forgotten by the whole world.

[2] "Only a Flower." Used by permission of Abingdon Press.

He took a stone and scratched upon the wall of his cell, "Nobody cares." A tiny green shoot came up one day through a crack in the stone floor. It reached up toward the light of the tiny window of the cell. The prisoner watered it with part of the water given him each day by the jailer. It grew until it became a plant with a beautiful flower. Then the prisoner crossed out the words he had written and wrote above them, "God cares."

A man walking over a Scottish moor picked up a tiny moss cup. He began to examine it under a pocket lens. A shepherd saw what he was doing and asked to see the flower through the glass.

"Can this be a moss cup?" he exclaimed. "I wish you had never shown it to me!"

"Why?" asked the man.

"Because I tread on thousands of them every day," the shepherd replied.

The perfection of a lovely flower and the sweetness of its fragrance comforts the heart and stirs longings for growth within the soul. We pray with the poet:

> God who touchest earth with beauty,
>   Make me lovely too,
> With thy spirit re-create me,
>   Make my heart anew.[3]

[3] Mary S. Edgar, "A Youth's Prayer." Used by permission.

Let Us Learn to Love the Stars

Men have studied the stars for thousands of years, and yet each year new marvels are being revealed. There seems almost no limit to further knowledge which is yet to be gained from these far-off, awe-inspiring worlds of the heavenly firmament. There are books today about the stars which are easy enough to make the study a delight. A visit to a planetarium or an observatory puts the study far ahead.

One evening I went to a friend's house. I found her stretched out on the ground with a little boy on either side of her, a pillow under their heads and a blanket over them, studying the stars. This particular evening they were watching for meteorites.

We are oppressed at times by the uncertainties of the days in which we live. We wonder if there is much we can depend on. In these moments it is good to go out into the silence of the night and lift our eyes to the shining heavens. We know the friendly stars are there and that God's hand holds them to their appointed places. We can be sure that he still rules his universe.

> In reason's ear they all rejoice,
> And utter forth a glorious voice;
> Forever singing as they shine,
> The hand that made us is divine.

Rachel Carson, eminent marine biologist, writes:

Those who dwell among the beauties and mysteries of the earth are never alone or weary of life. Whatever the vexations of their personal lives, their thoughts can find paths that lead to inner contentment and to renewed excitement in living. Those who contemplate the beauty of the earth find reserves of strength that will endure as long as life lasts. There is symbolic as well as actual beauty in the migration of the birds, the ebb and flow of the tides, the folded bud ready for the spring. There is something infinitely healing in the repeated refrains of nature—the assurance that dawn comes after night, and spring after winter.[4]

Let us open nature's vast book before us, and follow in awe and wonder her paths which lead to God.

PRAYER:

Eternal Father, give us, we pray thee, eyes to behold the wonder of thy creation. May we hear thy voice in the song of the birds and the flowing of the stream. May we see thy face in the glory of the sunset, and the still radiance of a star. Inspire within our hearts new reverence for the Giver of all life and beauty. In Christ's name we ask. AMEN.

[4] Copyright © 1956 by Rachel L. Carson. Reprinted by permission of the author.

OUT IN THE FIELDS WITH GOD

The little cares that fretted me,
  I lost them yesterday,
Among the fields, above the sea,
  Among the winds at play,
Among the lowing of the herds,
  The rustling of the trees,
Among the singing of the birds,
  The humming of the bees.
The foolish fears of what might pass
  I cast them all away
Among the clover-scented grass
  Among the new-mown hay,
Among the husking of the corn
  Where drowsy poppies nod,
Where ill thoughts die and good are born—
  Out in the fields with God!

AUTHOR UNKNOWN

VESTIGIA

I took a day to search for God,
And found Him not. But as I trod
  By rocky ledge, through woods untamed,
  Just where one scarlet lily flamed,
I saw His footprint in the sod.

Then suddenly, all unaware,
Far off in the deep shadows, where
  A solitary hermit thrush
  Sang through the holy twilight hush—
I heard His voice upon the air.

And even as I marveled how
God gives us Heaven here and now,

35

In a stir of wind that hardly shook,
The poplar leaves beside the brook—
His hand was light upon my brow.

At last with evening as I turned
Homeward, and thought what I had learned
    And all that there was still to probe—
    I caught the glory of His robe
Where the last fires of sunset burned.

Back to the world with quickening start
I looked and longed for any part
    In making saving beauty be . . .
    And from that kindling ecstasy
I knew God dwelt within my heart.[5]

BLISS CARMAN

[5] Reprinted by permission of Dodd, Mead & Company from *Bliss Carman's Poems*. Copyright 1929 by Bliss Carman. Also used by permission of McClelland & Stewart Ltd.

CHAPTER IV

A Crown of Devotion

SCRIPTURE: Mark 1:32-35

HYMNS: "Take Time to Be Holy"
"Dear Lord and Father of Mankind"
" 'Mid All the Traffic of the Ways"

MEDITATION:

There was an old German professor whose
life was a benediction to all who knew him.
His students were determined to find the
secret of it. One night some of them hid in
his study where the old man usually spent
his evenings. It was late when the teacher
came in and he was very tired. He opened his
Bible and spent an hour studying it. Closing
it, he bowed his head and said, "Well, Lord
Jesus, we're on the same old terms."

This is the secret and the crown of great
lives, to know God, and to be conscious of
his daily presence in our lives. Rufus Jones
said, "The purpose of religion is to make a
person conscious of the presence of God.
There are many paths to this end—great art,
nature, music, truth, great literature, poetry,

37

and the unselfish acts of men. But the final climb is the path of prayer.''

We develop a consciousness of the reality of God in our lives when we follow three paths: daily study of his Word, daily prayer, and daily meditation.

Bible Study

To help us to develop an awareness of God, we turn first to God's written word. He speaks to us in it. It is God in print. The Bible is not as difficult to understand as many people think. God will open its meaning to us in answer to our needs and our desire to know.

Edward P. Blair tells of a little mud-walled, thatched-roof church in China where a missionary once told the story of the prodigal son. He described the old home, the far country, the loneliness of the wanderer, and the pain and then joy in the father's heart. When he finished, an illiterate peasant woman, who had heard the story for the first time, leaned over and asked the minister's wife, ''How did the preacher find out about my boy?''

The men and women of the Bible are as human as you and I. We see in them our own struggles and sins. We hear God's voice speaking to us as he did to them, wooing us to righteousness. In Jesus' life and words we find all the answers to life's problems.

God's word hidden in our hearts gives us a sense of his presence. It lifts us over the hard places in life.

Many years ago when surgical operations were not as common as now and more dangerous, I became fearful over the necessity of such an experience. I was terrified over the possibility of leaving my three little children should the outcome prove fatal. After sleepless nights I sought help in God's Word. In Ps. 57:1-2, I read:

Be merciful unto me, O God, be merciful unto me: for my soul trusteth in thee: yea, in the shadow of thy wings will I make my refuge, until these calamities be overpast. I will cry unto God most high; unto God that performeth all things for me.

I felt that God was beside me. All fear left me and did not return. I felt securely held in God's love, and I knew that whatever came was best for me and for my children.

We are safe indeed when we can say, "He that dwelleth in the secret place of the most High shall abide under the shadow of the Almighty."

Prayer

In order to abide in God we must learn to pray.

39

Walter Rauschenbusch, the prophet of social righteousness, says:

Men can be classified in many ways. You can classify them as rich and poor, as strong and weak, as capable and stupid, as moral and immoral. But perhaps one of the profoundest classifications would be the division of mankind into men who truly pray, and men who do not.

Most of us at one time or another "say our prayers." But do we really pray? George Buttrick says, "Prayer is friendship with God." Friendship is an intimate relationship. It is the intercourse between two persons based on love and trust and loyalty. This intercourse is not expressed always in words. Sometimes it consists alone in the quiet consciousness of each other's presence. Sometimes it is felt in the yearning of one heart for the other.

One day the late Bishop Thoburn sat on shipboard talking to an atheist. Finally the man asked, "But how do you know that Jesus Christ is alive today?" The Bishop replied, "Because I talked with him this morning in my stateroom."

When this friendship exists between man and the eternal God, vast powers are released in the world. Man becomes a channel through which the life of God moves among men. He becomes victorious in his own spiritual life, and a blessing to those about him.

Meditation

If prayer is talking to God, meditation is listening for God to talk to us. Meditation is the quiet time, the time of waiting and listening for him to speak. God can speak only when we are quiet. Jesus usually chose a quiet time for communion with his Father. It was in the early morning, or in the silent dark hours of the night that he gave himself to meditation. And he usually chose a quiet place—the desert, a hilltop, a garden. He told his disciples, "Enter into thy closet and when thou hast shut thy door, pray to thy Father." It is the shut door which shuts out the world, and shuts God in.

In George Bernard Shaw's *Saint Joan,* Charles the king is complaining to Joan, "Why don't the voices come to me? I am the King, not you." Joan replies: "They do come to you, but you do not hear them. You have not sat in the field in the evening listening for them. When the Angelus rings you cross yourself and have done with it; but if you prayed from your heart, and listened to the trilling of the bells in the air after they stop ringing, you would hear the voices as well as I do."

One evening the poet Archibald Rutledge

was walking through the South Carolina woods and he met an old Negro who was on his way to church. After a little talk, the old man said, "Now I must go and light my candle at His fire."

As we draw near to our Lord in loving daily devotion by prayer and Bible reading and meditation, we light our feeble candles at his fire and go forth to carry the light to a dark world.

PRAYER:

O God, our Father, we thank thee for thy Holy Word which reveals thy laws unto us. We thank thee for thy Son, our Saviour, who reveals thyself to our hearts. Give us the deep experience in prayer which leads us into thy presence where we may commune with thee. We adore thee, we praise thee, we love thee! May we carry the atmosphere of devotion into every walk of life, reminding others of thee. Forgive the weakness of our past endeavors and hasten the work of thy divine spirit within us. To the honor and glory of thy name. AMEN.

Let us labor for an inward stillness,
An inward stillness, and an inward healing;
That perfect silence where the lips and heart
Are still, and we no longer entertain
Our own imperfect thoughts and vain opinions.

42

But God alone speaks in us, and we wait
In singleness of heart, that we may know
His will, and in the silence of our spirit
That we may do His will, and do that only.

HENRY W. LONGFELLOW

THE SANCTUARY

I love to come to this still place
  Where deeper peace is always found.
  To kneel as though on holy ground,
And feel my Master face to face.

I do not know how I could live
  If there were not this refuge sweet,
  Where I could linger at His feet
And He to me sweet healing give.

But He will only let me stay
  Until His peace has lifted me
  Up where the dying world I see.
And then He sweetly bids, "Away!"

And I have found if I would keep
  His presence with me all day through,
  Then I must learn His will to do;
And in His harvest fields to reap.

O Christ, Thou Lover of all men,
  Thou unseen Presence ever near,
  Create within me ears to hear,
And grant me eyes that see. Amen.[1]

RALPH S. CUSHMAN

[1] Copyright 1936 by Ralph S. Cushman. Used by permission of Abingdon Press.

THE VISION OF CHRIST

Have you and I today
Stood silent, as with Christ, apart from joy or fray
Of life, to see by faith His face
And grow by brief companionship more true,
More nerved to lead, to dare, to do
For Him at any cost? Have we today
Found time in thought our hand to lay
In His and thus compare
His will with ours and wear
The impress of his wish? Be sure
Such contact will endure
Throughout the day, will help us walk erect
Through storm and flood; detect,
Within the hidden life, sin's dross, its stain;
Revive a thought of love for Him again;
Steady the steps which waver; help us see
The footpath meant for you and me.

GEORGE KLINGLE

CHAPTER V

A Crown of Thorns

SCRIPTURE: John 12:20-32

HYMNS: "Must Jesus Bear the Cross Alone?"
"Are Ye Able?"
"Saviour, Thy Dying Love"

MEDITATION:

There is a story which has been retold many times, but whose message is ever fresh and poignant. It is of an incident which happened when the body of Abraham Lincoln was lying in state in Cleveland on its journey back to his home in Illinois. An old Negro woman, leading a little child by the hand, stopped in line to look for a long time at the face of the great emancipator of her race. She stooped and whispered to the child, "Take a long, long look, honey, that man died for you."

We need to take a long, long look just now at the crown of thorns, because it is the symbol of that One who died for us.

An old Scottish minister once said, "All life's crowns are crowns of thorns." Is this

true for all of us? If so, what does this crown
of thorns hold in store for those who wear it?

The True Test of Discipleship

First, see how Jesus made willingness to
bear a cross the true test of discipleship. He
said, "If any man will come after me, let
him deny himself, and take up his cross, and
follow me." It was Jesus' own way of life.
He accepted it of his own free will, not because he had to do it. He called his followers
to do the same.

Cross-bearing to the Christian means some
burden, some trial, some suffering he accepts
for himself that God's purpose may be
furthered in the world. It was in this spirit
that the four heroic chaplains on board the
"Dorchester" gave their life belts to save
the lives of other men, and went down with
the torpedoed ship in the icy waters of the
North Atlantic. It is not likely that at the
moment these men ever calculated their risk.
They did not hesitate to put their own
chances last. They were predictable men.
There was only one thing they could do, and
that was to put the other man first.

Such a way of life responds to every moment of crisis, of decision, of opportunity by
self-forgetfulness and self-giving. It is self-
lessness. It is the way of the cross.

46

Cross-Bearing Releases Power

Not only is cross-bearing something over and above that which is thrust upon us, but it releases a power in the world that never could be released otherwise.

When we assume responsibilities, tasks, burdens, over and above what is required of us, for the furtherance of God's plans, we are able to achieve results we never could obtain in our own strength.

Our hearts grow warm at the thought of Robert Louis Stevenson, tied to his bed by sciatica, suffering a terrible hemorrhage, and then afflicted with ophthalmia which threatened him with permanent loss of sight, when his wife said to him bitterly, "I suppose you will say, as usual, that things have fallen out for the best, if only we look at them in the right way?"

"Why now," he answered, "it's odd you should say that, for that's exactly what I have been thinking. What I needed was a rest, and this has forced me into it."

On another day when cramp in both arms would not let him write, and, taking to dictation, his voice flickered and went out, he fell back on the deaf and dumb alphabet until his hands failed through weakness. But all the time he kept on writing articles so gallant, so full of joy of life, that the sheer splendor of his courage has strengthened other men down to this present day.

I quote the famous Scottish minister Arthur John Gossip:

If Christ carried His cross, then so must I; if He gave His life, here is mine too. The faith is not an opiate but a spur, an inspiration, a compulsion to do more, far more than we have ever seen before to be our duty. The whole meaning of the thing is to create a world at last of spirits like Christ, flinging their lives away for God and others in His joyous and unreckoning way; and you and I among them. And if we don't wish that, then Christ is not for us.

Cross-Bearing Brings Us into Closer Fellowship with Christ

When we make a new acquaintance, if happily we find we have a common background, or have come from the same part of the country, or have known some of the same people, our interest kindles, and our friendship begins to grow. There is a deeper understanding between people who may have followed the same road, and whose experiences have paralleled each other's.

So it seems to be in our relationship with the Master. Our fellowship deepens as we walk with him and share his experiences. One who knew him well exclaimed, "That I may know him and the fellowship of his sufferings.''

Perhaps few have shared Christ's life more perfectly than Nicolas Herman of Lorraine, known to most as Brother Lawrence. He was a lay brother living in an early Christian monastery in the seventeenth century. In one of his letters he wrote:

There is not in the world a kind of life more sweet and more delightful, than that of a continual walk with God; those only can comprehend it, who practise and experience it. . . . Be not discouraged by the repugnance which you may find to it from nature; you must do yourself violence. . . . You must go on, and resolve to persevere in it till death, despite all difficulties.

Cross-bearing is never easy, but its reward is closer fellowship with our Lord.

Let us stand before his cross on Calvary and take a long, long look. "This man died for you."

PRAYER:

O Thou who giveth to thy children more than they can ask or think, grant to take out of our hearts the loves and the things which keep us from the full understanding of thy will. Inspire within us a desire for union with thee which is greater than any other love. May we lose all selfish ambitions and all selfish habits which blind us to greater ends found only through free intercourse with thee. Help us not to be afraid to pay the price of complete self-giving. Draw our hearts to thee by the power of thy great love. Through Jesus Christ, our Lord. AMEN.

O, the bitter shame and sorrow,
    That a time could ever be,,
When I let the Saviour's pity
Plead in vain, and proudly answered,
    "All of self, and none of Thee."

Yet He found me; I beheld Him
    Bleeding on th' accursed tree,
Heard Him pray, "Forgive them Father!"
And my wistful heart said faintly
    "Some of self, and some of Thee!"

Day by day His tender mercy,
    Healing, helping, full and free,
Sweet and strong, and ah! so patient,
Brought me lower, while I whispered,
    "Less of self, and more of Thee!"

Higher than the highest heavens,
    Deeper than the deepest sea,
Lord, Thy love at last has conquered,
Grant me now my supplication,
    "None of self, and all of Thee!"

THEODORE MONOD

OBEDIENCE

I said, "Let me walk in the fields,"
    He said, "No, walk in the town."

50

I said, "There are no flowers there."
  He said, "No flowers, but a crown."

I said, "But the skies are black.
  There is nothing but noise and din."
And He wept as He sent me back,
  "There is more," He said; "there is sin."

I said, "But the air is thick,
  And fogs are veiling the sun."
He answered, "Yet souls are sick,
  And souls in the dark undone."

I said, "I shall miss the light,
  And friends will miss me, they say."
He said, "Choose to-night
  If I am to miss you, or they."

I pleaded for time to be given.
  He said, "Is it hard to decide?
It will not seem hard in heaven
  To have followed the steps of your Guide."

I cast one look at the fields
  Then set my face to the town,
He said, "My child, do you yield?
  Will you leave the flowers for the crown?"

Then into His hand went mine,
  And into my heart came He;
And I walk in a light divine
  The path I had feared to see.

                              GEORGE MACDONALD

51

CHAPTER VI

A Crown of Life

SCRIPTURE: John 11:20-45

HYMNS: "Look Ye Saints! The Sight Is Glorious"
"For All the Saints Who from Their Labors Rest"
"Ten Thousand Times Ten Thousand"

MEDITATION:

Eugene O'Neill wrote a play called *Lazarus Laughed*. In it he tells of the new Lazarus who returned from the grave after Jesus raised him from the dead. There is an irresistible, never-failing joy about him which breaks forth in rippling laughter. Men hear it and follow him. Nothing defeats him any more. Finally the emperor of Rome burned him at the stake because of his own inability to still this maddening laughter. Lazarus went to his death with laughter floating out upon his followers. The secret was that he had found out in his experience of death that we need have no fear of it. He shouts: "There is only life! I heard the heart of Jesus laughing in my heart! Fear is no more! There is no death! Death is dead! There is only laughter!"

But fiction is not enough. We seek authority in the quest for this crown. We look to Jesus as the only one who ever returned from the grave to speak with authority upon immortality. Just what did he say?

Jesus Showed That God Will Be There

Before Jesus came, the idea of what the future life might hold was vague and shadowy, even ghostly at times. But Jesus said that it is a home which he is preparing for us where we shall be with him and with those we love.

"In my Father's house are many mansions: if it were not so, I would have told you. I go to prepare a place for you. And if I go and prepare a place for you, I will come again, and receive you unto myself; that where I am, there ye may be also."

Not only did Jesus comfort his disciples with this promise, but he promised the same to the penitent thief on the cross when he said to him, "To day shalt thou be with me in paradise."

To be with Him! If we had no other words than these, they are enough to satisfy all our longings.

At one time my work kept me over two thousand miles away from home. Only once

53

a year could I manage a visit. After the first pleasure of being a part of the family again was over, the one thing I wanted above all was to be near my mother. It wasn't necessary to talk. Just to sit beside her, to look into her eyes, to feel her presence, was all that mattered. Each hour and each day were like physical things in my hands that I felt I never could let go.

To be with Him! That will be a home coming far dearer than anything we cherish on earth. We shall enter into the joy of our Lord.

Jesus Showed That Eternal Life Begins Here but Continues

When Jesus comforted Martha after Lazarus had died, he said to her, "I am the resurrection and the life: he that believeth in me, though he were dead, yet shall he live: And whosoever liveth and believeth in me shall never die."

He wanted her to know that God made his children for life, not death, and life, once begun upon this earth, is immortal life. It survives the loss of the physical body only to enter a new and greater existence.

Bishop Arthur J. Moore tells the story of the little son of Louis XVI of France, who was placed in prison after the execution of his mother and father. He was surrounded by evil men who tried to teach him vulgar and vicious words and thoughts. But when they would suggest an evil thought or coarse word the child would stand at full height and say, "No, I cannot do that. I cannot say that, for I was born to be a king."

The Bishop reminds us that

the followers of the Christ way were not born for fifty, or seventy, or eighty years of struggle for bread. They were born the sons of God, the comrades of Him who was born to be the King of Kings, of Him who holds the keys of death and hell and the grave. His message is "Be not afraid of death, be not afraid of what follows death." He has been the whole way through and stands on the other side in His resurrected power and glory.

Jesus Showed That God Counts Every Human Soul As Precious

We may rest assured that our destiny is safe in our Father's hands because each one of us is precious to him. Jesus reminded his disciples that two little sparrows are worth only a very little, but that God notices when even one of them falls on the ground. Then he said, "Fear ye not therefore, ye are of more value than many sparrows."

This belief is expressed in wonderful words by George Buttrick:

55

Through all the ages the elect of God have always felt that He would not blow out a life as if it were a candle. Nor do we believe that He, having power to make us capable to immortal longings, has no power to give us the immortality for which we long. How can they deem it possible—those who have known God—that He has mocked His children with a dream of eternity?

When my son died in early manhood, I knew then that if I had ever had any doubts about immortality, or if I had never believed in it at all, I would have to believe in it now. God could never waste a young life such as his with its promise of leadership and service to the world. Such a life must find its fulfillment—if not here, then in another life. There was never any room in my heart for doubt after that.

PRAYER:

God, our Father, who art our refuge and strength, we thank thee for the hope of immortality which is within us. We thank thee that the resurrection of Jesus confirms this hope. Direct our steps aright as we make the journey of life, and bring us at last to thee. We pray in Jesus' name. AMEN.

CAUSE

Without the night
We could not dream

How beautifully
A star may gleam.

Without the dark
We could not know
How tenderly
A moon may glow.

And without death
We could not guess
How immortality
May bless.[1]

JANE MERCHANT

They are not lost who find
The sunset gate, the goal
Of all their faithful years.
Not lost are they who reach
The summit of their climb,
The peak above the clouds
And storms. They are not lost
Who find the light of sun
And stars and God.[2]

HUGH ROBERT ORR

'TIS LIFE BEYOND

I watched a sail until it dropped from sight
Over the rounding sea—a gleam of light,
A last, far-flashed farewell, and, like a thought
Slipt out of mind, it vanished and was not.

[1] Copyright 1954 by Abingdon Press. Used by permission.
[2] "They Softly Walk." Used by permission.

Yet, to the helmsman standing at the wheel,
Broad seas still swept beneath the gliding keel;
Disaster? Change? He left no slightest sign,
Nor dreamed he of that dim horizon line.

So may it be, perchance, when down the tide
Our dear ones vanish. Peacefully they glide
On level seas, nor mark the unknown bound.
We call it death—to them 'tis life beyond.

AUTHOR UNKNOWN

CHAPTER VII

A Crown of Witness

SCRIPTURE: Matt. 5:14-16

HYMNS: "I Love to Tell the Story"
"Jesus Calls Us"
"Hark, the Voice of Jesus Calling"

MEDITATION:

One night a noted artist appeared in the Hollywood Bowl. He gave a performance of superb music with a technique near perfection. Behind the musician the shadow of a man fell upon the shell of the bowl. Although the audience was moved by the music, the people were watching the shadow on the shell.

The shadow of a man! Nothing about him is quite so important. It is his witness, his influence which reaches out and touches those around him.

Jesus' last words were, "Ye shall be witnesses unto me both in Jerusalem, and in all Judea, and in Samaria, and unto the uttermost part of the earth."

And the ancient prophet Daniel has said that these witnesses who turn many to righteousness shall shine as the stars, forever and ever.

You Witness by the Kind of Person You Are

In a court of law the only man who will be accepted as a witness is one who has firsthand information. He must know the accused, or have evidence of what transpired.

We can witness for the Master only when we know him personally, when our experience with him is firsthand. When Jesus called his disciples, he said, "Follow me, and I will make you fishers of men." The condition was that they follow him. They must live with him, learn of him, and become the kind of person he was. Then the personal goodness of their lives speaks for itself. It is what is often called the "contagion of character."

Bishop Matthew W. Clair has told of an old fisherman who had a faith that was simple and sure. Someone asked him why he believed in the risen Christ. He said: "Do you see those cottages near the cliff? Well, sometimes when I am far out to sea, I know that the sun is risen by the reflection in those windows."

The very best witness to our faith in Christ is the way we reflect him in our characters. He will draw men unto himself when he is lifted up in our lives. When men see the living spirit of Christ in us, they see an authentic witness.

You Witness by What You Do

The way we conduct our business, the manner in which we run our homes, or the pattern of our recreations—all are a witness before the world of what the gospel means to us.

A man gave the credit of his conversion to Christianity to a timid old man who lived near him. When hearing it, the old man looked puzzled and replied, "I can't remember ever saying much to you about becoming a Christian."

"No," said his friend, "you didn't have much to say about it, but you lived me to death. I could stand all their preaching and upset all their arguments, but I couldn't stand the way you lived."

"Let your light so shine before men, that they may see your good works, and glorify your Father which is in heaven," said the Master.

You Witness by Passing on the Good News

One need not go to the far-off places of the earth to spread the gospel. He can carry the story of Jesus to others wherever he is and under all circumstances. If the blessed story is your best-loved topic of conversation, if it is your favorite message in writing, your first choice in reading, and your constant theme in song, it will be diffused like fragrance about you, everywhere you go.

By means of inspired literature we may carry the message into hospitals, prisons, army camps, everywhere there is need. None is better than the little *Upper Room* devotional magazine with daily meditations. It is read by millions and has won countless numbers to Christ. The authors and readers of this little booklet represent every major evangelical denomination. Stories of spiritual victories come from its readers all over the globe. A former editor of the booklet gave these:

A German schoolteacher in Durlach found an *Upper Room* which American soldiers had left while occupying her house during the war. She wrote: "It gave me strength and courage in these dark and sad days of our life."

A police chief in a Texas town walked down a Methodist aisle and asked, without previous notice, to be received on confession of faith. His name was Levi Miller. Shortly afterward he died suddenly. As friends went through the papers on his desk, they found an *Upper Room;* the corner of a page for the week preceding his decision for Christ was turned down. The meditation was based on the call of the first Christian named Levi.

Thus the printed word may become the channel for our witness to many lives in the Master's name.

PRAYER:

Our Father, we thank thee for the blessed gospel of thy dear Son which has been ours since childhood. May we so live and work that we may be worthy witnesses to it. Forgive us our negligence in telling the story to a needy world. We rededicate ourselves to thy service in the name of the One who gave his life for all men everywhere. AMEN.

HARVEST

Up, and be doing! The time is brief.
And life is frail as the autumn leaf.
The day is bright and the sun is high,
Ere long it will fail from the glowing sky;
The harvest is ripe and the fields are wide,
And thou at thine ease mayest not abide.
The reapers are few and far between,
And death is abroad and his sickle keen.
Go forth and labor! A crown awaits
The faithful servant at heaven's gates;
Work with thy might ere the day of grace
Is spent, ere the night steals on apace.
The Master has given His pledge divine,
"Who winneth souls like the stars shall shine."

AUTHOR UNKNOWN

MY MASTER

I had walked life's path with an easy tread,
Had followed where comfort and pleasure led;
And then by chance in a quiet place
I met the Master, face to face.

With station and rank and wealth for a goal,
Much thought for the body, but none for the soul,
I had thought to win in life's mad race,
When I met the Master, face to face.

I had built my castles and reared them high,
Till their towers had pierced the blue of the sky;
I had vowed to rule with an iron mace,
When I met the Master, face to face.

I met Him and knew Him, and blushed to see
That eyes full of sorrows were turned on me;
And I faltered, and fell at His feet that day,
While my castles melted away—

Melted and vanished, and in their place
I saw nought else but my Master's face;
And I cried aloud, "O, make me meet
To follow the path of Thy wounded feet!"

And now my thoughts are for the souls of men,
I've lost my life, to find it again,
E'er since that day in a quiet place
I met the Master face to face.

AUTHOR UNKNOWN

64

CHAPTER VIII

A Crown of Sorrow

SCRIPTURE: Heb. 2:9-10
            Jer. 10:19
            Matt. 26:36-46

HYMNS: "I Know Not What the Future Hath"
         "In the Hour of Trial"
         "O Love, Divine, That Stooped to Share"

MEDITATION:

A crown of sorrow? How can that be? you ask. Strange it may be, but there is a way to meet sorrow when it comes which will reveal a glory in it. I am thinking of sorrow in the larger sense, not only of bereavement. Anything which brings us sadness, misfortune, frustration, or trouble holds the hope of this hidden glory.

Jesus is the noblest example of this way to meet sorrow. We read that he was made perfect through suffering and thereby crowned with glory and honor.

How may we discover this glory at the heart of suffering?

Accept Sorrow

First we must learn to accept sorrow.

When trouble comes, if we open our hearts to it without resentment or bitterness, it will work within us a strange alchemy. Through it we will bring a blessing to others. "All sorrow nobly borne tends to uplift the world."

E. Stanley Jones tells of a Christian who, at the round-table conference, gave this as his view of what religion meant to him in experience: "If you follow Christ three things will happen to you. First, you will be delivered from all your fears. Second, you will be absurdly happy. Third, you will have trouble." Stanley Jones concludes: "You cannot be delivered from all your fears, nor can you be absurdly happy unless you have learned to accept trouble and use it."

Senator and Mrs. Leland Stanford lost their only son while in Europe on a pleasure trip. He was just entering manhood and was beautiful in face and form. Their vast fortune was to have been his.

They were in Florence, Italy when he was stricken with typhoid fever. When he died, Senator Stanford lost consciousness from grief and shock. As soon as he regained consciousness, he uttered the words so often repeated at the time: "Now the children of California will be our children." Returning to America, Senator and Mrs. Stanford founded and endowed Stanford University, that other young men might have an education and training.

When we accept sorrow, we make it possible for God to heal the wound. If we resent it, we cause it to fester in the heart and to embitter the whole life.

Share Your Sorrow

Then secondly, you need, if possible, to share your sorrow with some friend or friends. The fact that sorrow is shared relieves the burden. If the friend can do no more than listen, the tension is lessened and the heart comforted.

A Negro went to the desk of one of the secretaries at Riverside Church in New York, where Harry Emerson Fosdick was pastor at that time. He said, "My wife has just died, and all the stars have gone out of my sky. Can I see Dr. Fosdick?"

A few minutes before, the secretary had, of necessity, refused to allow an important person to see Dr. Fosdick. But to the imploring Negro the secretary said, "I will try to arrange it." In a few minutes he was admitted to the study. A half hour later he came out, his face aglow. On his way out he stopped at the secretary's desk and said very quietly, "He put the stars all back. It is light again."

The friend of all friends is our heavenly Father. Tell your grief to him. Pour out your heart to him. Realize that he will understand completely. And then listen after you talk to him. He will show you how to meet your problem. He will give you power to overcome it.

Grow Through Your Sorrow

Let us go one step farther and realize that sorrow has a mission. We cannot escape it, but we can be changed by it. We can grow into a deeper understanding of and deeper sympathy for other people's griefs. We may become gentler, braver, more patient. We may develop a deeper faith.

A missionary family—father, mother, and three children—were all murdered in China, in what was known as the Vegetarian Riots. Four of the other children escaped after they saw the rest of the family murdered. These four met again and decided what their revenge would be: They would all go and get the best training possible and then return to China and give their lives in service for those who had murdered the rest of the family. They did so, and spent years of fruitful, loving service to the land that had been so unjust to them. One of these brothers won to Christ Dr. James Yen, who became the father of the Mass Educational Movement in China.

This movement taught hundreds of thousands of Chinese to read.

Sir Oliver Lodge said, "As we rise in the scale of existence we find ourselves actually choosing pain and trouble rather than comfort and ease. The highest kind of pain is voluntary; it is suffering for a cause, or for the sake of others."

Jesus said in his last prayer with his disciples, "For their sakes I sanctify myself." Can we say those words?

"For their sakes" I forget my own loneliness, that my children may be happy.

"For their sakes" I do not complain of pain, that those near me may be happy.

"For their sakes" I do without some luxury, that I may give to ones in need.

"For their sakes, I."

PRAYER:

Loving Father, thou knowest the sorrows of our hearts. Thou knowest the answer to each one. Grant us courage and peace that we may be brave to meet each day. Give us enough courage for one day at a time. Show us how to rise through our sorrows to more glorious life. In Jesus' name. AMEN.

> It was a thorn,
> And it stood forlorn
> In the burning sunrise land:

A blighted thorn
And at eve and morn
Thus it sighed to the desert sand:

Every flower,
By its beauty's power
With a crown of beauty is crowned;
No crown have I.
For a crown I sigh,
For a crown that I have not found.

Sad thorn, why grieve?
Thou a crown shall weave,
But not for a maiden to wear;
That crown shall shine
When all crowns save thine
When the glory they gave are gone.

For thorn, my thorn,
Thy crown shall be worn
By the King of Sorrows alone.

OWEN MEREDITH

If all the skies were sunshine
Our faces would be fain
To feel once more upon them
The cooling plash of rain.
If all the world were music
Our heart would often long
For one sweet strain of silence
To break the endless song.
If life were always merry
Our souls would seek relief

And rest from weary laughter
In the quiet arms of grief.[1]

HENRY VAN DYKE

PAIN

The cry of man's anguish went up to God,
"Lord, take away the pain!
The shadow that darkens the world Thou hast
made;
The close coiling chain
That strangles the heart: the burden that weighs
On the wings that would soar—
Lord, take away the pain from the world thou
hast made
That it love Thee the more!"
Then answered the Lord to the cry of the world,
"Shall I take away pain,
And with it the power of the soul to endure,
Made strong by the strain?
Shall I take away pity that knits heart to heart,
And sacrifice high?
Will ye lose all your heroes that lift from the fire
White brows to the sky?
Shall I take away love that redeems with a price,
And smiles with its loss?
Can ye spare from your lives that would cling
unto mine
The Christ on his Cross?"

AUTHOR UNKNOWN

[1] From *The Builders*. Used by permission of Charles
Scribner's Sons.

71

CHAPTER IX

A Crown of Gold

SCRIPTURE: Acts 3:1-11

HYMNS: "Saviour, Thy Dying Love"
"O for a Heart to Praise My God"
"Walk in the Light"

MEDITATION:

Peter, the disciple of Jesus, was a rich man. There was no precious metal in his pocket, but he possessed a finer kind of wealth. He gave to the beggar at the temple gate wealth that all the money in the world could not buy. He said to him, "Silver and gold have I none; but such as I have give I thee: In the name of Jesus Christ of Nazareth rise up and walk." And he took him by the hand and lifted him up. And the man leaped up and walked and praised God.

Jesus himself was not very much interested in material gold. He saw too many dangers in it. He did not teach that a man to be good must be poverty-stricken. He did say, "How hardly shall they that have riches enter into the kingdom of God!" Jesus regarded a

man's bank account as one of the accidents
of his life. He saw that there are other riches
of greater importance. What are these?

A Man Is Rich by What He Stands For

A person may have little in his bank account, but if he keeps his honor clean and his
integrity pure, he is rich. The one who is
above reproach in business, whose personal
life is pure, whose word can be trusted, and
whose justice can be counted upon, has true
wealth.

Sir Walter Scott spent his large earnings
in enlarging and beautifying his estate, Ab-
botsford, on the river Tweed. He was about
to retire as a country gentleman. Suddenly
he was faced with bankruptcy and a debt of
100,000 pounds through the indiscretion of
his partners in business. He wrote in his
diary: "I feel neither dishonored nor broken
down by the news I have received. I have
walked my last in the domain which I have
planted; sat for the last time in the halls I
have built, but death would have taken them
from me if misfortune had spared me. Dis-
couragement is to me a tonic and a bracer."

Rising at four every morning he wrote the
famous Waverley novels to pay his debts.
They were written anonymously so that no
one might know he was paying off his debts
in such a manner. Sir Walter Scott's books

reflect the nobility of his stainless spirit. His integrity of character has enriched the world as largely as his immortal writings.

A Man Is Rich by What He Shares

Our lives become rich in proportion as we share them with others. Every burden we lift and every service we render comes back to bless our own lives. The prophet long ago said it this way, ''Cast thy bread upon the waters: for thou shalt find it after many days.'' The modern poet wrote:

> Is thy cruse of comfort wasting?
> Rise and share it with another.
> And through all the years of famine
> It shall serve thee and thy brother.
>
> For the heart grows rich in giving—
> All its wealth is living gain;
> Seeds which mildew in the garner
> Scattered fill with gold the plain.

ELIZABETH CHARLES

Ebenezer Scrooge had plenty of money in the bank on that lonely Christmas eve when he was visited by the spirits of the Past, Present, and Future. But he was poverty-stricken in everything that made life good and beautiful.

Then on Christmas morning he awoke to a new appreciation of the world and everything in it. Shouting, "Merry Christmas to all," he went out to buy the goose for the Cratchit's dinner. Good will overflowed in his heart and hands.

Jesus told us to store our treasure in heaven and not in barns on earth. This treasure is made up of good works done for him here. In the Revelation we read of those who have gained the heavenly life, "and their works do follow them."

A Man Is Rich by What He Loves

There is no substitute in life for a warm and loving heart. "Though I bestow all my goods to feed the poor, and though I give my body to be burned, and have not charity [or love], it profiteth me nothing."

Our world is vastly richer because of the warm and loving heart of Toyohiko Kagawa. As a young lad he prayed, "O God, make me like Christ." His whole life became a channel through which the love of God flowed out into the world.

Living in wretched poverty in the slums of Kobe, he poured that love into the lives of thousands of paupers, outcasts, and criminals, sharing his food and bed with them.

While he was still in seminary, Kagawa adopted a beggar baby to keep it from starving and nursed it to life. We hear him sing of this little one:

My God is Love;
My God is Love,
Tender and deep;
I feel His close sweet presence
Looking down to see
The beggar-baby
Lying in my arms asleep.[1]

Kagawa is the glowing example of the apostle Paul's words: "As sorrowful, yet always rejoicing; as poor, yet making many rich; as having nothing, and yet possessing all things."

Integrity of character, active service for others, and outgoing love for all mankind are the true riches of any life. They compose a crown that fadeth not away.

PRAYER:

Dear Father, what may we render thee for the riches of thy grace which thou hast given us through thy Son, our Lord and Saviour? Show us how to evaluate true riches that our lives may abound in love and good works. Help us to reflect thy glory in our everyday living. Enable us to go forth strong in thy love, to live worthily for Thee. In the name of thy dear Son we pray. AMEN.

[1] Used by permission of Abingdon Press.

A child's kiss
Set upon thy sighing lips shall make thee glad;
A poor man served by thee, shall make thee rich;
A sick man helped by thee, shall make thee strong;
Thou shalt be served thyself by every sense
Of service which thou renderest.

ELIZABETH B. BROWNING

UNANSWERED PRAYERS

I thank Thee, Lord, for mine unanswered prayers,
  Unanswered, save Thy quiet, kindly, "Nay,"
Yet it seemed hard among my heavy cares
  That bitter day.

I wanted joy: but Thou didst know for me
  That sorrow was the lift I needed most,
And in its mystic depths I learned to see
  The Holy Ghost.

I wanted health; but Thou didst bid me sound
  The secret treasuries of pain,
And in the moans and groans my heart oft found
  Thy Christ again.

I wanted wealth; 'twas not the better part;
  There is a wealth with poverty oft given,
And Thou didst teach me of the gold of heart,
  Best gift of Heaven.

I thank Thee, Lord, for these unanswered prayers,
  And for Thy word, the quiet, kindly, "Nay."
'Twas Thy withholding lightened all my cares
  That blessed day.

AUTHOR UNKNOWN

A MORNING PRAYER

Let me today do something that will take
  A little sadness from the world's vast store
And may I be so favored as to make
  Of joy's too scanty sum a little more.

Let me not hurt, by any selfish deed
  Or thoughtless word, the heart of foe or friend;
Nor would I pass, unseeing, worthy need,
  Or sin by silence when I should defend.

However meager be my worldly wealth,
  Let me give something that shall aid my kind—
A word of courage, or a thought of health
  Dropped as I pass for troubled hearts to find.

Let me tonight look back across the span
  'Twixt dawn and dark, and to my conscience
    say—
Because of some good act to beast or man—
  "The world is better that I lived today." [2]

ELLA WHEELER WILCOX

[2] Used by permission of Rand McNally & Co.

CHAPTER X

A Crown of Friendship

SCRIPTURE: Phil. 4:1-4
Rev. 3:20

HYMNS: "What a Friend We Have in Jesus"
"I've Found a Friend"
"Blest Be the Tie That Binds"

MEDITATION:

A woman said to me one day in speaking of another woman: "She is the sort of person I would love to have for a friend," and I answered, "One would be rich to have her friendship."

Nearly everyone is hungry for friendship. As John Donne puts it, "No man is an island." We cannot live alone. We crave an answering comradeship. We need hands that reach out to clasp our own, eyes that kindle into ours, and voices to answer when we call.

In speaking of his dearest friends at Philippi, Paul calls them "my joy and crown," and those who "shine as lights in the world."

What is it that makes friendship so great a treasure?

Friendship Helps Us Live Unselfishly

A true friend is ever seeking to serve the one he loves. No effort is too great, no sacrifice too dear to give. He does not forget the daily expression of his concern and devotion. He continually travels the second mile for his friend in surprising little acts of love.

My daughter had had an unusually difficult week. After putting her children to bed on Friday night, she fell into bed wishing for nothing in all the world but sleep. Opening her eyes the following day, she saw with alarm that it was nearly noon by the clock. Rushing to her baby's room, she found the crib empty; then in her little boy's room she found the same. Her friend next door had quietly come in the early morning and taken the children to her own home for bath and breakfast and play so that my daughter might have undisturbed rest.

This gift of friendship had nothing to do with material things. It was a gift of self much more valuable. It asked for nothing in return except that it might continue to serve in quiet, loving ways.

Friendship Stimulates Our Growth

Our friends help us to live at our best. They give us an incentive for growing mentally and spiritually. They inspire us to live up to their expectation of us. They arouse in us the inner stimulus without which growth is impossible.

One of the great friendships of my life came to me when I worked in an office under a remarkable man many years my senior. His vast sum of knowledge inspired me to enroll in a Chautauqua reading course in order to increase my own meager knowledge. His flawless diction sent me to the dictionary for the exact meaning of every doubtful word that I read or heard. His beautiful Christian character made me long to possess every Christian grace.

Such friendship is beyond price. It gives one a goal toward which to strive. It enlarges and enriches life.

Friendship Opens the Way to Christ

The nobility of earthly friendships points us to the Friend above all friends. Jesus opened the door to this friendship when he said, "I have called you friends." This fellowship with him raises friendship to its highest level. It is an intimacy which will never leave us lonely. It is a comforting presence which will take away our sorrows, and a strengthening power which will make us adequate for whatever life may bring.

A little Indian boy on the ballground of a Christian settlement in the Far West was heard to exclaim after an exceptionally good hit, "Parum, Yesuswami, parum!" which in his own language is, "Look, Lord Jesus, look!"

We, too, may experience this feeling of the presence of the Master with us. We can have this friendship when we seek it with all our hearts.

Have you heard Christ say, "Behold, I stand at the door and knock: I will come in and sup with you"?

Can you imagine what such friendship would mean? Only two of you at the table. Everything that matters most to you matters to him. He has the answers to all the perplexing problems that confront you. He will give you strength to meet them. He will travel beside you in never-ending friendship.

PRAYER:

Teach me, my Father, to be a friend to all who need me. Help me to see thy image in every man and to be understanding and patient and loyal in my dealings with him. May my own friendship with the Master point men to thee. In Jesus' name. AMEN.

> My debt to you
> Is one I cannot pay
> In coin of any realm
> On any reckoning day;
> For where is he can figure
> The debt when all is said,

Of one who made you sing again
When all dreams were dead.
Or where is the appraiser
Who shall the claim compute
Of one who made you sing again
When all the songs were mute.

FRANK CRANE

FRIENDSHIP

If all the friends I've made on earth,
Could gather 'round my humble hearth,
And pledge their love to me anew,
And ask for mine—what would I do?
I'd thank each for a lesson taught
And love each for the love he brought;
Try to give with grateful heart
More than my share—to do my part.
But to the One who cares for all,
Who yearns o'er e'en a sparrow's fall,
My prayers go forth to Heaven's blue,
For, lo, dear friends, He gave me you!
The sunshine, flowers, the gentle rain,
All seem more lovely since you came;
He gave me you with friendship fine,
He gave me you, and the *world is mine!*

CHRISTINA ROSSETTI

83

CHAPTER XI

A Crown of Joy

SCRIPTURE: Phil. 4:1-7
> Acts 16:12-34

HYMNS: "Joy to the World"
> "When Morning Gilds the Skies"
> "Let All on Earth Their Voices Raise"

MEDITATION:

"A man is about as happy as he makes up his mind to be," said Abraham Lincoln.

A crown of joy is one of the easiest of all crowns to find if we make up our minds to look for it. Jesus wore this crown. The words, "Be of good cheer," were often upon his lips. He moved among men with laughter and warmth of spirit. He entered into their happiness at glad festivals such as the marriage feast at Cana. Every sight and sound of beauty in nature and in his fellow men drew forth his joy.

But Jesus' joy was more than happiness. It went deeper than laughter. It was a part of his relationship with his Father. Hebrews speaks of his going to his death "for the joy that was set before him." On the last night before his crucifixion, he bequeathed this joy to his disciples. He said, "My joy I leave with you." He left it to us. Whence comes this crown?

Doing the Day's Work Well

In the first place, such joy comes from right living. The man who lives in right relation to God and to his fellow men has no guilt complexes to trouble him, no vain regrets to taunt him. His memories are sweet. He is at peace with God and with himself.

Charles L. Allen, in his book *When the Heart Is Hungry,* tells a story about a boy who asked a farmer for work. The farmer asked him if he were willing to work and if he could be trusted. The boy replied, "Please sir, yes sir, I can sleep well on a windy night." The farmer thought him to be a little foolish, but he hired him. All went well until one night a heavy storm came up. The farmer ran to awaken the boy, calling, "Come quickly, we must tie down the haystacks, and secure the tools, and lock up the barn doors." But the boy slept so soundly the farmer gave up and ran out to do the work himself. In the fields he found the haystacks all tightly tied down, the tools were in a safe place, and the doors were securely locked. He understood then what the boy had meant. He could sleep well on a windy night because he had done his work well.

The boy in this story was a faithful steward of the talent God had given him. His talent might not have been very much, but he used what he had to the best of his ability. He earned the Master's words, "Well done, good and faithful servant. Enter thou into the joy of thy lord." When we consecrate what we have to God and seek to do our best, we enter into this joy. This joy satisfies the heart. It rests the spirit. Then no matter how high the winds nor how furious the storm the joy remains.

Appreciating Everyday Blessings

Joy comes from being aware of and appreciating the little everyday blessings of life. It is a fact that some of us are always waiting for something big to happen to make us happy—something out in the future, such as a legacy, a trip, some new possession. But life is not made up of special happenings alone. It consists of the routine affairs of the ordinary day in the home, in the office dealing with homely everyday duties. If we are to be happy we must find it in these simple pursuits.

Agnes Turnbull, in her book *Dear Me*, says:

There is only one thing about which I shall have no regrets when my life ends. I have savored to the full all the small daily joys—the bright sunshine on the breakfast table, the fragrance of white lilacs, the light rains that start gently after midnight, the hour when the family comes home, Sunday evening supper before the fire. I have never missed one moment of beauty, nor ever taken it for granted—Spring, Summer, Autumn, Winter. I wish I had failed as little in other things.

The warm friendships which are a part of our daily lives can bring us abiding joy if we do not take them for granted. They may be family or neighborhood friends. They may sometimes be the friends we meet within the pages of great books.

A minister tells of a charming elderly lady who lived alone. One day he asked her if she was ever lonely. She smiled and answered, "Why should I be?" She pointed to a small bookcase and said, "Those are old friends of mine. How wisely and well they talk! Then I am surrounded by loved ones I knew long ago. I also have my flowers, birds, and cat, all of which are my friends. And of course, I often talk to my heavenly Father. No! I am never lonely."

Jesus said, "I have called you friends; for all things that I have heard of my Father I have made known unto you." He invites us into the inner circle of his friendship, where we may share his thoughts and feelings. Here we will find the secret of victorious joyful living.

Trusting in God

Such friendship with God is based upon our trust in him. This is true of any friendship. If I do not have any faith in your sincerity, or if I doubt your loyalty, I cannot be your friend. But if I know deep within me that you are the person you seem to be, then I rejoice because I have found a true friend. To discover this relationship with the eternal God is above all joys.

Paul and Silas were in the inner prison at Philippi with their feet fast in the stocks. They had been beaten and their clothes taken away. They had every reason to complain. Instead they prayed and sang praises to God at midnight. Their joyful trust in God brought about their speedy release from prison and the conversion of their jailer and his whole family.

This triumphant joy is shown in the trust of a poor Methodist woman of the eighteenth century:

I do not know when I have had happier times in my soul than when I have been sitting at work with nothing before me but a candle and a white cloth, and hearing no sound but that of my own breath,

with God in my soul and heaven in my eye. . . .
I rejoice in being exactly what I am, a creature
capable of loving God, and who, as long as God
lives, must be happy. I get up and look for a
while out of the window, and gaze at the moon
and stars, the work of an Almighty hand. I think
of the grandeur of the universe, and then sit
down, and think myself one of the happiest be-
ings in it.

Trust in God brings joy because it releases
us from fear and loneliness. We are never
alone with our problems and losses. We may
not understand experiences that come, but we
know that God is always good. We can trust
the future in his hands.

PRAYER:

Our Father, wilt thou show us the path
of life, for in thy presence is fullness of joy,
at thy right hand there are pleasures for
evermore. AMEN.

THE WORD FOR TODAY IS JOY

Today, whatever may annoy,
The word for me is joy, just simple joy!
The joy of life;
The joy of children and wife;
The joy of bright blue skies;
The joy of rain; the glad surprise
Of twinkling stars that shine at night.
The joy of winged things upon their flight;

The joy of noon-day and the tried
True joyousness of eventide;
The joy of labor, and of mirth;
The joy of air and sea, and earth—
The countless joys that ever flow from Him
Whose vast beneficence doth dim
The lustrous light of day,
And lavish gifts divine upon our way.
    Whate'er there be of Sorrow,
    I'll put off till Tomorrow.
And when Tomorrow comes why then
'Twill be Today and Joy Again! [1]

JOHN KENDRICK BANGS

THE ROAD AHEAD

The road behind is lost amid the shadows
That hide our failures with their kindly gloom.
The road ahead is mystically flaming,
As sudden glory fills the earth and skies,
With rainbow promises that are proclaiming
Though crushed and broken, Hope can never die.

So lift our hearts in glad rejoicing
And fare forth to meet the splendor of the dawn
With happy singing and with wings upon our feet.
Let no one voice regret and sorrow for what is gone,
Because somewhere along the road ahead
We shall find all our dreams we thought were dead. [2]

EDGAR DANIEL KRAMER

[1] Used by permission of the estate of John Kendrick Bangs.
[2] Used by permission.

CHAPTER XII

A Crown of Love

SCRIPTURE: Luke 10:25-37
John 21:15-17

HYMNS: "There's a Wideness in God's Mercy"
"Love Divine, All Loves Excelling"
"Blest Be the Tie That Binds"

MEDITATION:

What! You haven't any star—and you're going on the sea?

You're going into battle with no music?

You're going on a trip without a book?

What! You have no love and yet you talk of living?

The search for this crown is of the greatest importance because if we are really to live we must learn to love.

When do the beauties of nature stir your heart to ecstasy? When you love them.

When do little children bring you glimpses of God? When you love them.

When do the sufferings of others enlarge your sympathies and call forth your devotion? Only when you love the sufferers.

91

Would you know life's deepest lessons and greatest joys? Then you must learn to love. But how?

God's Love Is Boundless

First, we must be sure of God's love. We must know that God himself is love—that he is always loving, always good. His love transcends all earthly love at its best. It is boundless.

A minister from England was on the ocean with his little seven-year-old daughter coming to America. That morning on shipboard he had preached on the love of God. It had been a difficult service because he had lost his wife just a few weeks before.

As he and the little girl leaned upon the rail of the ship gazing upon the vast expanse of sea, the child said to him, "Daddy, does God love us as much as we love Mummy?"

"He does," said her father. "God's love is the biggest thing there is."

"How big?" asked the child.

"How big? I'll tell you. Look across the sea. Look up. Look down. God's love is so big it stretches around us farther than all this water. It is higher than the blue sky above us. It is deeper than the deepest part of the ocean beneath us."

After a moment of silence the little girl suddenly grasped her father's arm, exclaiming, "Daddy, we're right in the very middle of it!"

Yes, we are in the center of God's love. We have been taught all our lives that God loves us. But when trouble strikes, sometimes we seem to forget. We ask, "Why did God send this upon me? Why is he punishing me?" God never wills evil for his children. He built this world on moral principles, and when these laws are broken men suffer. But God loves and sustains his children through their suffering if they will let him. "As the heaven is high above the earth, so great is his mercy toward them that fear him." We will be strong for the battles of life when we feel that God cares, and that underneath are the everlasting arms.

There Must Be No Limits to Our Love

As God's love is boundless, so we must set no limits to our interest and concern for others. We will learn to love when we include all men in our hearts. There is a sort of love which includes only our own family, our friends, "our kind of folks." Beyond this little circle we feel very little interest or responsibility. Jesus expects more. He expects a long-range love—a love that includes the foreigner, the unresponsive, the ungrateful person. He expects us to love even our enemy, and the enemies of our country.

During the Armenian massacres of the last century, a town in Armenia was invaded by the Turkish army. In one home all the members of the family were killed except the daughters, who were carried off by the Turkish officers. One of the young girls escaped and eventually made her way to England. There she studied nursing, and was later placed in a British army hospital in Crimea.

One night, as she made the rounds of her patients, she was stunned to find in one bed the young Turkish officer whom she had seen kill her parents and brothers. His life was now in her hands. A little neglect and he would not survive. Instead she nursed him back to health. After he was well, he said to her, "I know who you are, and I know that you know me. Why did you not let me die when it was within your power to do so?"

She answered, "I am a Christian. Our Master said, 'Love your enemies. Do good to them which hate you.'"

He replied, "I did not know there was a religion like that. I would like to learn more about such a religion."

This kind of love is the love that Jesus showed upon the cross when he prayed, "Father, forgive them; for they know not what they do." It is the kind which comes through prayer and companionship with the Master. The spirit of Christ within our

94

hearts makes it possible for us to love our enemies and to forgive them. We cannot do it by ourselves alone.

We Learn to Love Through Practice

Practice is the test of love. It deepens as we put it into action. After his resurrection Jesus asked Simon three times if he loved him. Each time to Peter's protesting devotion he said, "Feed my sheep. Feed my lambs." In effect he was saying, "Prove it. Go and do something about it in daily life."

A story is told of the late Will Rogers when he was working on a Hollywood movie set. He went into a lunchroom and sat down at a counter beside a small Negro boy. After giving his order, Rogers remembered something he had forgotten. He left abruptly without waiting for his order. The little Negro boy turned and said, "He wouldn't sit beside me."

Someone told the actor what the boy had said. The next day Will Rogers came into the lunchroom and found the boy. He bought a quart carton of ice cream. Then he and the little boy sat on the edge of the pavement and together they ate the entire quart of ice cream.

The love in Will Roger's heart for "even the least of these" made it necessary for him to seek out this little one and erase the hurt he had unknowingly inflicted. This is the test of true love.

"Lovest thou me?" Simon Peter heard these words from the Master's lips. Across the years we hear them speaking to our hearts.

"Lovest thou me"—enough to overlook the slights and hurts of daily life?

"Lovest thou me"—enough to forgive and forget the real wrongs we suffer at the hands of others?

"Lovest thou me"—enough to include persons of other races in our circle of friends?

"Lovest thou me"—enough to serve others instead of serving ourselves?

PRAYER:

Our Father, we ask that thou wilt increase thy love in our hearts. We can ask for nothing greater. Give us more of the love that shone forth in the life of Jesus. It alone can solve all our problems and bring thy kingdom on earth. Move within us in such fullness that our heart and hands may continually overflow with loving service to all mankind. In Jesus' name. AMEN.

LOVE

Love is the filling from one's own
    Another's cup;
Love is the daily laying down

And taking up;
A choosing of the stony path
   Through each new day
That other feet may tread with ease
   A smoother way.
Love is not blind, but looks abroad
   Through other eyes;
And asks not, "Must I give?" but
   "May I sacrifice?"
Love hides its grief that other hearts
   And lips may sing;
And burdened walks, that other lives
   May buoyant wing.
Hast thou a love like this
   Within thy soul?
'Twill crown thy life with bliss
   When thou dost reach the goal.

AUTHOR UNKNOWN

IF I HAVE NOT LOVE

Men send their speech across blue miles of space,
Across great continents their words ring clear,
Yet all their eloquence does not efface
The mountain barriers of hate and fear.
Men chart the heavens' mysteries, have explained
The atom, given their bodies to be burned
In war's fierce hells; and yet have never gained
The good for which their hearts have always
   yearned.

And I—ah, well indeed, dear Lord, I know
That all that I can say, or think, or do
Is utter nothingness, an idle show,
If I have not deep love, sincere and true;

97

Love for thy loveliness in star and tree,
Love for my fellow men, pure love for thee.[1]

JANE MERCHANT

THE COMMON OFFERING

It is not the deed we do,
   Though the deed be ever so fair
But the love the dear Lord looketh for,
   Hidden with holy care
   In the heart of the deed so fair.

The love is the priceless thing,
   The treasure our treasure must hold,
Or ever the Lord will take our gift,
   Or tell the worth of the gold,
   By the love that cannot be told.

Behold us, the rich and the poor,
   Dear Lord, in Thy service drawn near;
One consecratest a precious coin,
   One droppeth only a tear;
Look! Master, the love is here.

HARRIET McEWEN KIMBALL

[1] Copyright 1954 by Abingdon Press. Used by permission.

CHAPTER XIII

A Crown of Contentment

SCRIPTURE: Phil. 4:8-13

HYMNS: "My Times Are in Thy Hand"
       "Be Still My Soul: the Lord Is on Thy
          Side"
       "My Jesus, As Thou Wilt"

MEDITATION:
  My crown is in my heart, not on my head,
  Not deck'd with diamonds and Indian stones,
  Nor to be seen: my crown is call'd Content.

              WILLIAM SHAKESPEARE

Seekers of this crown are in quest of a
spiritual goal, an experience of the mind and
heart. We are all seekers of this treasure
and yet few find it. We may look in vain for
it among the material things of the world. It
is not made of gold or diamonds or Indian
stones. It is fashioned of a flower called
heart's ease, and is found in the heart.

Contentment Is a Way of Thinking

Helen Miller Lehman says:

Some people say, "If I were elsewhere, or living

99

under different conditions, I'd be happy." So few are ready to say, "Here where life has placed me, and with conditions as they are, I am very contented."

Contentment does not depend upon what we have, or where we are, or who our friends are, or what our job is. It is a state of mind; a mental outlook; the quality of our evaluation of our environment. Two persons may live under identical circumstances. One is happy, the other is discontented. The difference? The outlook of each upon life, and what he considers to be important. The happy man thinks what he has is important. The unhappy man thinks what he lacks is of greatest value. Lacking the things which seem of greatest value to him, he is discontented and unhappy.[1]

The writer of the above lines tells of a trip she made down the west Coast of Mexico where in an isolated spot she saw real contentment.

A Mexican man, his wife, and twelve children are the caretakers of a small fishing camp. They live in the most primitive conditions with few possessions and with the simplest fare. Yet these people possess poise, dignity, and gentle charm. And above all else they are happy.

The oldest son, Julio, who has talent as a sculptor, is ambitious and makes every effort

[1] "Soy Muy Contento," *P.E.O. Record*, April, 1952.

to improve himself. Yet when he was asked if he would like to come to the United States to study, he replied, "No, here I am very contented. In United States too much hurry, too much money, nobody happy. Here, everybody happy. Happiness is good."

Contentment Comes with Acceptance

Happiness and contentment depend upon our willingness to recognize and accept the things in our lives which cannot be changed. There are a few of these things in every life. Perhaps God has put them there for a purpose which we cannot yet understand. So let us give up fretting and trust him.

God has set some limits around each life. He has given each his own talent, his own physical inheritance and cultural background. Some of these we may improve and some we must live with. An old Japanese saying puts it this way:

The sign says, "Do not pick the blossoms."
This is useless against the wind which cannot read.

We must learn to accept ourselves, our children, our surroundings, when the choice of these lies in God's hands alone. Then we shall have peace of mind and release for joy in our own place in life.

I saw him across the dingy street
  A little old cobbler, lame, with a hump,

Yet his whistle came to me clear and sweet,
  As he stitched away at a dancing pump.
Well, some of us limp while others dance;
  There's none of life's pleasures without alloy,
Let us thank Heaven then for the chance
  To whistle while mending the shoes of joy.[2]

Contentment Comes from Leaving the Outcome in God's Hands

A firm faith in our Father's will for us takes away resentment and bitterness of heart when life grows difficult. It gives us the power to bear patiently any trial. We are able to leave the outcome in God's hand, knowing that it will be right. Paul said, "Godliness with contentment is great gain."

I am thinking of a fine person whose busy life of teaching was suddenly cut short by a severe heart attack. He was ordered to bed for many months. Later he wrote to me:

This being in bed has been a mountaintop experience. I saw spring come through my bedroom windows. I saw the whole miracle of the lilac tree; then the coming of the humming birds and the brilliant butterflies, and the wondrous beauty of the creek maples and now the oaks. At night I saw the heavens studded with diamonds and knew God was near me. I was never away from his love and care. My bed-resting was a blessed privilege. I know I am richer than I have ever been.

[2] From *The Great Texts of the Bible,* ed. J. Hastings. Used by permission of T. & T. Clark.

Paul found content even in prison because of his faith in God. He wrote: "Not that I speak in respect of want: for I have learned, in whatsoever state I am, therewith to be content. I know both how to be abased and I know how to abound; everywhere and in all things I am instructed both to be full and to be hungry, both to abound and suffer need. I can do all things through Christ who strengtheneth me."

We, too, may be happy in whatever state we find ourselves if we put our trust in our heavenly Father. Augustine said: "Our hearts are restless until they rest in Thee." And our Lord said, "Take no thought, saying what we eat? or, What shall we drink? or, Wherewithal shall we be clothed? Your heavenly Father knoweth that ye have need of all these things. But seek ye first the kingdom of God and his righteousness; and all these things shall be added unto you."

PRAYER:

> Dear God,
> I pray Thee for the grace
> To be content;
> Deep in my soul I pray;
> Great is my need!
> Not that I'd sit
> In shameful inactivity
> When bugles call to battle

For the right;
I fear not cowardice
In such an hour.
But this I pray—
That when the day is done,
And silence settles
O'er the battlefield,
That I may rest
In quietness with Thee,
May sit in sweet content,
May listen to the songs of Heaven,
Glimpse the eternal things,
Grasp the eternal power,
Remembering
The battle is the Lord's!
Thus would I be content.
O give Thy grace, dear God,
When heat of day is done,
That I may rest
In quietness with Thee,
Thy strength my strength,
Thy peace and joy mine, too,
Thy powers all
At last alive in me! [3] Amen.

RALPH SPAULDING CUSHMAN

Build a little fence of trust
   Around today;
Fill the space with loving deeds,
   And therein stay.

[3] In *Hilltop Verses and Prayers*. Used by permission of Abingdon Press.

A CROWN OF CONTENTMENT

Look not through the sheltering bars
  Upon tomorrow;
God will help thee bear what comes
  Of joy or sorrow.

MARY FRANCES BUTTS

A CONTRAST

Two men toiled side by side from sun to sun,
  And both were poor;
Both sat with children, when the day was done,
  About their door.
One saw the beautiful in crimson cloud
  And shining moon;
The other, with his head in sadness bowed,
  Made night of noon.
One loved each tree and flower and singing bird,
  On mount or plain;
No music in the soul of one was stirred
  By leaf or rain.
One saw the good in every fellow man
  And hoped the best;
The other marvelled at his Master's plan,
  And doubt confessed.
One, having heaven above and heaven below,
  Was satisfied.
The other, discontented, lived in woe,
  And hopeless died.[4]

SARAH KNOWLES BOLTON

[4] Used by permission.

105

CHAPTER XIV

A Crown of Thanksgiving

SCRIPTURE: Ps. 103

HYMNS: "When Morning Gilds the Skies"
"When All Thy Mercies, O My God"
"Joyful, Joyful, We Adore Thee"

MEDITATION:

In a beautiful ritual of the church the minister calls the people from the contemplation of God's mercy to the exercise of praise and thanksgiving. He calls them to the remembrance of what God did in Christ for them: "God so loved the world, that he gave his only begotten Son, that whosoever believeth in him should not perish, but have everlasting life." This is followed by the people's response: "Therefore with angels and archangels, and with all the company of heaven, we laud and magnify thy glorious name, evermore praising thee and saying: Holy, holy, holy, Lord God of hosts, heaven and earth are full of thy glory. Glory be to thee, O Lord most high! Amen."

Thus, from thinking about God's mercies

we are led to do something about it. "We move from faith to action."[1] Therefore with joyous hearts we enter upon this search.

Let Us Thank God for His Blessings

Praise is the constant mood of the true Christian. It should be unceasing.

There was once a law in some old monasteries that the chanting of praise should never cease. When one brother ceased, another took up his chant, and so it continued day and night. The mood of the heart, the attitude of the life, may be unceasing praise.

In Taylor Caldwell's *Tender Victory*, Johnny Fletcher, the young minister in the little mining town of Barryfield, declares:

If God had permitted us to live only one day to know that He is, that would have been enough for us. If He had allowed us to see one sunrise or one sunset that would have been more than enough. If in addition, He had granted us one hour of loving and being loved, how greatly has He blessed us! . . .

But He gave us still more. . . . He must give us the ultimate. He must walk among us as a man, in order to show us the way through our self-willed darkness and terror—the way to Him. He must die for us, and lift up His cross like a blazing light on the black hills of our sins.

[1] Bruce W. Ravenel.

107

For all our blessings let us give thanks. It is not possible to do so adequately. We can only try.

Let Us Thank God for the Evil as Well as the Good

Paul says that we should give thanks for everything. This includes the evil as well as the good. This is not always easy to do. Whatever God allows to come into our lives, we may ultimately find a blessing in it.

Do you remember the scene on the dark waters of the Sea of Galilee where those tossed-about fishermen were filled with fear because of the strange apparition moving toward them? "It is a spirit," they cried in terror.

Then above the storm came the reassurance of a beloved voice, "Be of good cheer; it is I; be not afraid." The dreadful visitant from an evil world, the awful calamity, turned out to be Jesus instead. With infinite gentleness he calmed their fears and spoke peace to their hearts.

So all our misfortunes turn out to be good fortune, and our losses turn into gains when we meet them with Jesus. And in the act of giving thanks for these seeming calamities, we find a new strength of character, a finer patience, a fresher charity. We cry, as someone has said, "O God, I thank thee for this gift. I thought it was a burden. Now I know it was thou, O Christ!"

Let Us Thank God by Our Lives

Thanksgiving that is real is expressed not only in words, but in deeds as well. When our hearts are humbled by God's blessings beyond all our deserving we express our debt in loving service to someone else. It was Anne Lindbergh who said, "One can never pay in gratitude; one can only pay in kind somewhere else in life." We who live in free America are worthy of our blessings only when we seek to do all in our personal power to bring these blessings to men everywhere.

Let us heed the warning given to the Hebrews of old:

Take heed lest when you have eaten and are full, and have built goodly houses and live in them, and when your herds and flocks multiply . . . lest you say in your heart, "My power and the might of my hand have gotten me this wealth." You shall remember the Lord your God, for it is he who gives you power to get wealth.

Let us hear also Jesus' words, "Everyone to whom much is given, of him will much be required."

PRAYER:

Gracious Lord, we thank thee for the blessings of our lives; the precious everyday blessings of home and family; the vast and glorious blessings of our nation. Help us to be good stewards of these gifts by sharing them with men everywhere. Make us ever mindful of the debt we owe to those who suffer and are in need. In Jesus' name we pray. AMEN.

Thou that hast given so much to me,
    Give one thing more—a grateful heart.
Not thankful when it pleaseth me
    As if Thy blessings had spare days;
But such a heart, whose pulse may be
    Thy praise.

GEORGE HERBERT

A THANKSGIVING PRAYER

For stars in every midnight sky,
For quivering glory in the grey,
For roses red—December grown,
For sunset at the end of day.
For the swift turning back to Thee
In joy or sorrow, peace or pain.
For the frustration of my plans
That mine might be the greater gain.
For graveyards that no terror hold,
For death which is the mask of life,
For love unaltered by the years.
For heart at rest in midst of strife.

110

For that best gift of all, Thyself.
For Thy dear Presence shining through,
And for Thy grace, Thy boundless grace,
Accept, O Lord, my thanks anew.[2]

RUTH WINANT WHEELER

THANKS BE TO GOD

I do not ask Thee, Lord,
That I have bread to eat while others starve;
Nor yet for work to do
While empty hands solicit heaven;
Nor for a body strong
While other bodies flatten beds of pain.
No, not for these things do I give thanks!

But I am grateful, Lord,
Because my meager loaf I may divide;
For that my busy hands
May move to meet another's need;
Because my doubled strength
I may expend to steady one who faints.
Yes, for all these do I give thanks.

For heart to share, desire to bear,
And will to lift,
Flamed into one by deathless Love—
Thanks be to God for this!
Unspeakable! His Gift!

JANIE ALFORD

[2] Used by permission.

CHAPTER XV

A Crown of Wisdom

SCRIPTURE: Matt. 2:1-12

HYMNS: "We Three Kings of Orient Are"
"There's a Song in the Air"
"Open My Eyes, That I May See"

MEDITATION:
> The Kings of the East are riding
>   To-night to Bethlehem.
> The sunset glows dividing,
> The Kings of the East are riding;
> A star their journey guiding,
>   Gleaming with gold and gem
> The Kings of the East are riding
>   To-night to Bethlehem.[1]
> > KATHARINE LEE BATES

These strangers from the East who came to Bethlehem seeking the holy child wore invisible crowns upon their heads, crowns of wisdom, more beautiful than the gifts they bore.

Two thousand years ago they were con-

[1] "The Kings of the East." Used by permission.

sidered to be men of wisdom. Today we still call them so. What were the sources of their wisdom?

They Recognized Their Need for God

First these were *seeking men.* They were searching for a new revelation of God. They were aware of the things of the spirit and they knew their hearts could never be satisfied short of a discovery of God.

The wise of all the ages have been the men who have cried out with Job, "How can I find God?" Creeds, dogmas, rituals are not enough. Man needs to talk to God and to hear him answer. "Let me speak, and answer thou me," prayed Job.

One evening during an electrical storm I heard my little boy crying, "I want my father. I want my father more than anyone else!"

"I want my heavenly Father" is the universal cry of the heart. One is wise indeed to recognize this need and to seek the answer. We pray with Augustine, "Thou hast made us for thyself and our hearts are restless until they rest in thee."

They Were Ready to Give Up All They Had to Find God

In the second place, these men were wise because they were willing to pay the price to find God. They were men of wealth and professional standing. They doubtless had everything in life to make it pleasant. But they left their families, their homes, their friends, to set out upon a fantastic journey which their friends could not understand. They were willing to accept the scorn and ridicule and the laughter, if need be. They were ready to pay the price in their search for reality.

When Benjamin Franklin was in his early twenties he and another young man started to learn Italian. They also started to play chess. Before long they were only playing chess. Franklin woke up to this; he refused to play any longer unless it were agreed that the loser should translate fifty pages of Italian before the game was resumed. Since they were well matched, they beat each other into a knowledge of Italian.

We hear Jesus saying, "If any man will come after me, let him deny himself." Whatever stands in the way of our search for him must be put aside. That is the price for wisdom.

They Fell Down and Worshiped Him

In the third place, these men were wise because when they found Jesus they fell down and worshiped him. They presented unto him their costliest gifts.

Only when the worship of God becomes an

integral part of us does life take on real meaning. When we open our eyes to him everywhere about us—in lovely nature, in needy humanity—we catch the meaning of it all, and we adore him.

A tiny boy of three was taken into an exquisite chapel by his grandmother. They stood silently within the door admiring the beauty of it. He whispered, pointing to the white and gold chancel, "Is that where people say their prayers?" Being told that it was, he slipped his hand out of hers and walked down to the altar. After touching each lovely object—the candlesticks, the chalice—he knelt before the chancel, bowed his head, and clasped his hands. After perhaps a whole minute of silence he rose and softly left the chapel.

If we are wise we will never lose the adoring worship of the child-heart. "Of such is the kingdom of heaven."

PRAYER:

O God, our Father, as the hart panteth after the water brooks, so pant our hearts for thee. Grant us wisdom to search for thee as the great Reality of life. Give us the courage and faith to put the unseen values of life above the seen. Draw near to us, and move within us that we may know we are thine. In the Saviour's name. AMEN.

ROYAL PRESENTS

The off'rings of the Eastern kings of old
Unto our Lord were incense, myrrh and gold;
Incense because a God; gold as a king;
And myrrh as to a dying man they bring.
Instead of incense (Blessed Lord) if we
Can send a sigh or fervent prayer to thee,
Instead of myrrh if we can but provide
Tears that from penitential eyes do slide,
And though we have no gold; if for our part
We can present thee with a broken heart
Thou wilt accept: and say those Eastern kings
Did not present thee with more precious things.

NATHANIEL WANLEY

WHO ARE THE WISE MEN?

Who were the Wise Men in the long ago?
  Not Herod, fearful lest he lose his throne;
  Not Pharisees too proud to claim their own;
Not priests and scribes whose province was to know;
Not money-changers running to and fro;
  But three who traveled, weary and alone,
  With dauntless faith, because before them shone
The Star that led them to a manger low.

Who are the Wise Men now, when all is told?
  Not men of science; not the great and strong;
  Not those who wear a kingly diadem;
Not those whose eager hands pile high the gold;
  But those amid the tumult and the throng
  Who follow still the Star of Bethlehem.

B. Y. WILLIAMS

CHAPTER XVI

A Crown of Hope

SCRIPTURE: Rom. 8:24-25
    Luke 2:25-35

HYMNS: "Whispering Hope"
   "God of Our Fathers, Known of Old"
   "Lead On, O King Eternal"

MEDITATION:
 Be thou the rainbow to the storms of life,
 The evening beam that smiles the clouds away,
 And tints to-morrow with prophetic ray!

          BYRON

There is an old-fashioned book which I sometimes read for the good of my soul. It is *Aunt Jane of Kentucky*. Aunt Jane is a very talkative person. One day, talking to her grandchild, she said, "Did you ever think, child, that nearly all the work we do keeps us looking down? Once in a while it's a good thing to stop work and look up at the sky. It gives you hope, and as long as you've got hope, child, you've got everything."

Jesus had a great deal to say about faith and love, but as far as I know he never mentioned hope. Was it unimportant to him?

117

No, because he lived it. His whole life was an example of constant hopefulness. His reliance upon his Father, his confidence in sinful men, his refusal to give up in the face of misunderstanding, and his never-failing courage reveal the power of a great hope in his life.

Hope is a driving force which is necessary for great living. Men must see the better day ahead if they are to grow individually and if the world is to progress toward a nobler life. Just what is it that hope gives to us?

Hope Keeps Us from Giving Up

As long as we hold on to hope we will not give in to despair over the mistakes we make and our failures to live up to the best we know. Our burdens will never become too great to bear, nor the future seem too dark to meet.

A woman went to call upon a sick friend who was complaining bitterly of her lot. The invalid asked her friend to give an account of what had happened to her in the years since they were in college together. The visitor gave a brief outline of a busy life. She told how she had gone from riches to poverty, had fought tuberculosis for twenty years, and was now facing blindness within two years. But she was still head of the woman's work in her church and intended, even after she became blind, to go right on doing some kind of useful work, and to meet whatever came with cheer.

The sick woman attributed her subsequent recovery more to the lift she received that day from her friend than to the doctors and the medicines she received.

"I will never give up hope," said a person I know, who was going through blinding experiences of trouble and grief; and in God's good time her prayers and dreams were answered.

Hope Helps Us Take the Long View

Our world today faces some of the most discouraging and difficult problems it has ever known. There seems to be plenty of room for fear and pessimism. In such a time it pays to take the long look. There have been times before which seemed to be the end of progress and civilization, but they have passed and the pendulum has swung upward again.

The old prophet Simeon, burdened by the weight of years and the oppression of his people still kept his eyes fixed upon the coming of the Promised One who was to redeem Israel. At last, when he held the infant Saviour in his arms, he saw from the mountaintop of vision the final goal of Christ's mission. He saw the breaking of the light that was to lighten the Gentiles and be the glory of his people Israel.

When we look back over history, we realize that no time is ever as bad as it seems to those living within it. It was Emerson who said, "This time, like all other times, is a very good one, if we know what to do with it." And someone else has said, "The trend of civilization is ever upward. We are in the Golden Age of the world so far."

Hope Helps Us Glimpse a
Better World of the Future

Today the world has the atomic bomb; it has the threat of advancing communism. But it also has the beginnings of world efforts for lasting peace. It has benevolences never before dreamed of in history. It has a new awakening of man's responsibility for brotherhood.

Four hundred years ago Lady Jane Grey sat in the Tower of London and wrote an immortal letter. It was on the eve of her execution, while life and love were still before her. Her letter to the Protestant leaders of England was this: "Fight manfully on," she wrote; "fight manfully on. Come life, come death, the loss of men is not the loss of the cause. The battle is God's. The victory ours."

Can we see a better world of tomorrow with enthusiasm such as this? In view of world conditions being as they are, it will depend upon our belief in God. If we believe that in spite of appearances God is always good, and that "above the storm the smallest pray'r will still be heard"; if we believe that God always has the final word, then we will not give way to doubt and fear. The mind and spirit of our Lord was one of hope. We, too, may rejoice in it.

PRAYER:

God of our fathers, give us courage to see that truth and goodness are on the march, and that the world is moving forward to richer understanding of what God means our lives to be. In Jesus' name. AMEN.

> Yet sometimes glimpses on my sight,
> Through present wrong the eternal right;
> And, step by step, since time began,
> I see the steady gain of man.

> JOHN GREENLEAF WHITTIER

BETWEEN MIDNIGHT AND MORNING

You that have faith to look with fearless eyes
  Beyond the tragedy of a world at strife,
And trust that out of night and death shall rise
  The dawn of ampler life;
Rejoice, whatever anguish rend your heart,

121

That God has given you, for a priceless dower,
To live in these great times and have your part
   In Freedom's crowning hour;
That you may tell your sons who see the light
   High in the heaven—their heritage to take—
"I saw the powers of darkness put to flight!
   I saw the morning break!" [1]

              SIR OWEN SEAMAN

For I dipt into the future, far as human eyes could
   see,
Saw the Vision of the world, and all the wonders
   that would be;
Saw the heavens fill with commerce, argosies of
   magic sails,
Pilots of the purple twilight, dropping down with
   costly bales;
Heard the heavens fill with shouting, and there
   rain'd a ghastly dew
From the nation's airy navies grappling in the
   central blue;
Far along the world-wide whisper of the south-
   wind rushing warm,
With the standards of the peoples plunging thro'
   the thunder-storm;
Till the war-drum throbb'd no longer, and the
   battle flags were furl'd
In the Parliament of man, the Federation of the
   world.

              ALFRED TENNYSON

[1] Reproduced by permission of *Punch*.

CHAPTER XVII

Wearing the Crown

SCRIPTURE: Matt. 23:1-12
Rev. 4:10-11

HYMNS: "My Jesus, As Thou Wilt!"
"When I Survey the Wondrous Cross"
"O Could I Speak the Matchless Worth"

MEDITATION:

"The saint that wears heaven's brightest crown in deepest adoration bends; the weight of glory bows him down the most when most his soul ascends; nearest the throne itself must be the footstool of humility."[1]

We have come now to the close of the meditations on the Christian graces, the practice of which places a crown upon the head of the one who is worthy to wear it.

These crowns are bestowed by Jesus, and are invisible to all but his eyes. But there is one mark which the ones who attain a crown have in common, and one which all men recognize. It is the grace of humility. Only these wear a crown whose hearts and lives

[1] J. Montgomery.

123

are centered not in themselves, but in God and their fellow men. There are many crowns, each precious in the sight of God, but only the humble in spirit wear them.

Jesus was deeply concerned over the lack of humility in the religious leaders of his time. He saw the lack of it even in his own disciples. He said: "He that is greatest among you shall be your servant. And whosoever shall exalt himself shall be abased; and he that shall humble himself shall be exalted."

The Difficulty of True Humility

It is always hard to be humble. Most of us are afraid to be humble. We are afraid of being overlooked or unappreciated. So we feel the need to build ourselves up.

My husband's mother dropped in to see us one day about noon. Immediately I began to tell her all I had accomplished that morning. I had gotten up early to get an early start. I had worked in the garden, I had done the housework, I had finished the ironing. I had prepared the evening meal in advance. On and on I paraded my accomplishments, until suddenly I realized what I was doing. I was trying to impress her with my virtues so that she might realize how fortunate her son was to have chosen the kind of wife he did. Instead I was doing just the opposite.

It boosts our ego to tell others about the good things we do. It also makes us feel important. Instead we might remember:

> If you're right take the humble side—
>> You'll help the other fellow.
> If you're wrong, take the humble side—
>> And you'll help yourself.[2]

The Measure of Humility

Phillips Brooks said, "The true way to be humble is not to stoop until you are smaller than yourself, but to stand at your real height against some higher nature, that shall show you what the real smallness of your nature is."

When we are tempted to take pride in some accomplishment, we have only to measure it by the greater ability of someone else and our sense of humility returns. Emerson said, "Every man I meet is my superior in some way. In that I may learn from him."

The great orchestra leader Toscanini was rehearsing a Beethoven symphony with his orchestra. When it was over, the men rose and applauded Toscanini. When the applause stopped, he said, "Men, do not applaud me. It is not I. It is Beethoven." After a mag-

[2] R. L. Irwin.

nificent performance, Toscanini still knew that the greater glory belonged to the master, Beethoven, and not to him.

Instead of looking at ourselves, let us study others and their gifts. It will enrich our own lives and sweeten our relationships with others.

The Test of Humility

We become humble by devoting ourselves to serving others. There is something divinely beautiful in the faithful humility of men and women who are content to serve their fellow men in inconspicuous ways and places—those who get the complaints and none of the praise.

Booker T. Washington one day arrived in a town to make an address. He was met at the station by a white cab driver, who, when he saw that his passenger was a Negro, refused to drive him to the auditorium. The time was short and it was necessary for the speaker to go at once. So Mr. Washington said: "All right then. You get in the rider's seat, and I'll drive you to the auditorium."

The bigger a man is the more ready and willing he is to perform the lowly deed of service. It was the Master himself who took the towel and bowl and washed his disciples' feet, saying, "If I then, your Lord and

Master, have washed your feet; ye also ought
to wash one another's feet."

PRAYER:

O Thou who art no respecter of persons, I thank
Thee that in Thy blessed Son, the carpenter of
Nazareth, Thou has come to seek and to save the
lost. I rejoice that at Thy feast the poor, the
maimed, the lame, the blind are welcome, for in
spirit I am all of these. Strip from me all pride
of place, of possession, of culture, of intelligence,
and of good works; make me and keep me humble
in Thy sight.

Our world cries out, O God, for humble, saintly,
self-giving Christians. Increase their number,
Lord, lest we perish in the haughtiness of our own
devices. In the name of the poor man who became
our Lord. Amen.[3]

GEORGIA HARKNESS

HUMILITY

Though heaven be high, the gate is low,
And he that comes in there must bow:
    The lofty looks shall ne'er
    Have entrance there.

O God! since Thou delight'st to rest
In the humble contrite breast,
    First make me so to be
    Then dwell with me.

THOMAS WASHBOURNE

[3] Used by permission of Abingdon Press.

Blest are the pure in heart,
For they shall see our God;
The secret of the Lord is theirs,
Their soul is Christ's abode.

Still to the lowly soul
He doth Himself impart,
And for His temple and His throne
Selects the pure in heart.

Lord, we Thy presence seek,
May ours this blessing be;
O give the pure and lowly heart,
A temple meet for Thee.

JOHN KEBLE